Adverse Possession First Supplement to the 2nd Edition

Adverse Possession

First Supplement to the Second Edition

Stephen Jourdan QC and Oliver Radley-Gardner

Bloomsbury Professional

Bloomsbury Professional
An imprint of Bloomsbury Publishing Plc

Bloomsbury Professional Ltd
41–43 Boltro Road
Haywards Heath
RH16 1BJ
UK

Bloomsbury Publishing Plc
50 Bedford Square
London
WC1B 3DP
UK

www.bloomsbury.com

British Library Cataloguing-in-Publication Data

A catalogue record for this book is available from the British Library.

ISBN: PB: 978 1 78451 253 8

Typeset by Phoenix Photosetting, Chatham, Kent
Printed and bound by CPI Group (UK) Ltd, Croydon, CR0 4YY

Preface

The confident predictions of the death of adverse possession made after the Land Registration Act 2002 remain unfulfilled, over 14 years after that Act came into force.

Adverse possession cases continue to occupy the Land Registration division of the First-tier Tribunal (Property Chamber), which has taken over the jurisdiction of the Adjudicator; there have been over 90 adverse possession decisions since 2010. Despite that, important issues about the interpretation of Schedule 6 to the 2002 Act remain unresolved, notably the question of whether the reasonable belief required by para 5(4)(c) needs to continue up to the date of the application to the Land Registry. Developments in Hong Kong are illuminating the doctrine of encroachment, a perplexing doctrine which may or may not now be based on adverse possession, although it was probably of different origin. New conceptual problems are being thrown up by the interaction between the 2002 Act and adverse possession, some of which the Law Commission intends to address in its proposed reforms which we discuss in this Supplement. Some areas of difficulty will, however, remain untouched by those reforms. The interaction between illegality and adverse possession continues to raise knotty issues, not least because the law of illegality has been in a state of development, and because of recent statutory intervention in residential squatting cases. The law of implied licences and unilateral permissions has been shaken up by the Privy Council. For reasons that are difficult to discern, there has been a recent rise of cases on adverse possession by the mooring of boats. Who knows what the future will bring.

This Supplement brings the main work, in its second edition, up to date to 31st May 2017.

Stephen Jourdan QC

Oliver Radley-Gardner

Contents

This Contents list reflects the Chapters that are covered by this Supplement, not necessarily all of the Chapters in the Second Edition.

Table of Cases

This Supplement aims to state the law at 31 May 2017

Abbreviations

Law Commission Consultation Paper 227, *Updating The Land Registration Act 2002* is Law Commission CP 227.

Chapter 1
Definitions and overview

1–08 The modern law is that the class of persons in whom the right to recover land is vested is not limited to those who are able to show that they have the benefit of a legal estate, relatively better than that of the squatter. It appears that a person with a sufficiently expansive licence, or a sufficiently expansive set of statutory rights and powers, may be in 'possession' or entitled to possession in the sense that he exercises, or has the right to exercise, control over the given piece of land. This raises issues about the effect of time running against persons whose rights arise out of statutory rights and powers, and whether such statutory rights and powers can be time-barred: as to these sorts of cases, see paragraphs 15–04A and following, below.

1–22 Add to Fn 45: see also *Chan Mei Lin v Lee Hong* [2015] HKCA 568 and *Tang Kai Tung v Tang Kai Lun* [2016] HKCA 171.

1–23 On 1 July 2013, the functions of the Adjudicator to Her Majesty's Land Registry were transferred to the First-tier Tribunal (Property Chamber) (Land Registration Division) and the Adjudicator to Her Majesty's Land Registry was abolished by article 4 of the Transfer of Tribunal Functions Order 2013. The Adjudicator and Deputy Adjudicators became judges of the First-tier Tribunal and in the case of the Adjudicator, also a deputy judge of the Upper Tribunal: see article 5. Transitional and savings provisions were made by Schedule 3 to that Order.

1–24 This paragraph was referred to by Deputy Adjudicator Owen Rhys in *Secretary of State for Transport v Quest Maidstone* REF/2010/0210 at [27]. He did not need to decide the point, but thought that where a person applied to land from one title, and becomes registered as proprietor of that land, any possession after the date of the application was immaterial, although he said: 'This area of uncertainty might be seen as a demonstration that the law relating to the limitation of actions does not always mesh comfortably with the law of land registration.' However, Deputy Adjudicator McAllister disagreed in *Abbs v Eldridge* REF/2010/1166 at [17]; she said: 'The determination of the question whether or not the Applicants (or the Respondents) are entitled to be registered as owners is not an action to recover land'. The point appears to be open to argument. The difference is whether the proceedings before the Adjudicator/First-tier Tribunal are actions to recover land and whether recovery of land entails the recovery of possession as a remedy. Judge Michael Mark would have agreed with the approach in *Quest Maidstone* in the first instance decision in *Port of London v Mendoza*

REF/2011/0751, at [25], though again it was not necessary to decide that point. In *Wilkin & Sons Ltd v Agricultural Facilities Ltd* REF/2011/0420 Edward Cousins, the Adjudicator to HM Land Registry concluded that 'the making of the application to the Land Registry to register an easement' constituted a 'suit or action' for the purposes of the Prescription Act 1832. He decided that the 'suit or action' was the making of the application and its acceptance by the Land Registry and not the decision by the Land Registry to refer the matter to the Adjudicator.

1–34A Morgan J provided the following useful list of principles in relation to adverse possession at [79] of *Balevents Ltd v Sartori* [2014] EWHC 1164 (Ch), being a retrial of [2011] EWHC 2437 (Ch) ordered by the Court of Appeal ([2012] EWCA Civ 1508).

(1) There is a presumption that the owner of land with a paper title is in possession of the land.
(2) If a person who does not have the benefit of this presumption wishes to show that he is in possession of the land, the burden is on him to show that he is in factual possession of the land and that he has the requisite intention to possess the land.
(3) For a person to show that he is in factual possession of the land, he must show that he has an appropriate degree of physical control of the land, that his possession is exclusive and that he has dealt with the land in question as an occupying owner might have been expected to deal with it and no-one else has done so.
(4) Whether a person has taken a sufficient degree of control of the land is a matter of fact, depending on all the circumstances; in particular the nature of the land and the manner in which such land is commonly enjoyed.
(5) The person claiming to be in possession may be in possession through his tenant or licensee, if that tenant or licensee has, on the facts, sufficient control of the land to amount to factual possession.
(6) The person seeking to show that he has had possession of land must show that he had an intention for the time being to possess the land to the exclusion of all other persons, including the owner with the paper title.
(7) The relevant intention is an intention to possess and need not be an intention to own.
(8) The intention to possess must be manifested clearly so that it is apparent that the person now claiming to have been in possession was not merely a persistent trespasser.
(9) If the acts relied on are equivocal then they will not demonstrate the necessary intention.
(10) It is possible in some cases for a person in possession to add to his own period of possession, the period of time during which his predecessor was in possession; this applies in particular where the predecessor relinquishes possession to a person who then takes possession.

Chapter 2
Historical introduction and proposals for reform

2–67A Morgan J has usefully summarised the pre-31 October 2003 law in relation to adverse possession as in *Balevents Ltd v Sartori* [2014] EWHC 1164 (Ch), as follows:[1]

> '80. Before the coming into force of relevant provisions of the Land Registration Act 2002 (on 13 October 2003), the law as to the acquisition of title by adverse possession in the case of registered land was governed by the Limitation Act 1980, sections 12 and 17 and schedule 1, and the Land Registration Act 1925, section 75. In summary, no action could be brought by a person to recover any land after the expiration of 12 years from the date on which the right of action accrued to him: section 12(1) of the 1980 Act. By paragraph 1 of schedule 1 to the 1980 Act, where a person bringing an action to recover land had been dispossessed or had discontinued his possession, then his right of action was treated as having accrued on the date of the dispossession or discontinuance. By paragraph 8(1) of schedule 1 to the 1980 Act, no right of action to recover land was treated as accruing until the land was in the possession of some person in whose favour the period of limitation could run; such possession was referred to in paragraph 8 as "adverse possession". By paragraph 8(2) of schedule 1 to the 1980 Act, where a right of action to recover land had accrued and after its accrual, before the right was barred, the land ceased to be in adverse possession, then the right of action should no longer be treated as having accrued and no fresh right of action should be treated as accruing unless and until the land was again taken into adverse possession. By section 17 of the 1980 Act, in the case of unregistered land, at the end of the period prescribed by the 1980 Act for any person to bring an action to recover land, the title of that person to the land was extinguished. This latter provision was modified in the case of registered land so that, instead of the registered proprietor's title being extinguished under the 1980 Act, his title was held on trust for the person who had, by virtue of the 1980 Act, acquired title as against the registered proprietor and that person could apply to be registered in place of the registered proprietor.

1 See too, the discussion of the Court of Appeal in *Parshall v Hackney* [2013] EWCA Civ 240, set out at paragraph 3–08 of this Update.

81. Thus, in relation to the period before 13 October 2003, applying the above law to this case, if it were shown that a person had been in possession of the disputed land for 12 years, then the registered proprietor of the disputed land, Birmingham City Council, would be unable to bring an action to recover possession of the land and the person who had been in possession for the relevant 12 years could apply to be registered as proprietor in place of Birmingham City Council.

82. As explained, the required period of adverse possession is 12 years. The provision in paragraph 8(2) makes it clear that the period of adverse possession must not be broken. In that sense, the possession must continue for 12 years. However, the concept of possession of land does not require a person to be physically present on the land for every moment of the 12 year period. With some types of land, a person can be in possession even if he is absent from it for long periods. The concept of possession is satisfied if the person claiming to be in possession for 12 years, without interruption, has had the requisite degree of control of the land throughout the relevant period of 12 years.'

2–71A The effect of the 2002 reforms has however, been conveniently set out in *Balevents Ltd v Sartori* [2014] EWHC 1164 (Ch) by Morgan J as follows:

'84. The relevant provisions of the Land Registration Act 2002 came into force on 13 October 2003. The 2002 Act introduced a different regime as to adverse possession in relation to registered land. However, schedule 12 to the 2002 Act contained transitional provisions. If a person had already been in adverse possession for 12 years prior to the coming into force of the 2002 Act, so that the registered title was held on trust for that person (under section 75 of the Land Registration Act 1925), then he remained entitled to be registered as the proprietor of the estate: 2002 Act, schedule 12 para. 18(1).

85. Subject to the transitional provisions of the 2002 Act, section 96 disapplied the earlier regime as to adverse possession in relation to registered land. Section 97 gave effect to the new regime contained in schedule 6. Paragraph 1(1) of schedule 6 allowed a person to apply to the registrar to be registered as the proprietor of a registered estate if he had been in adverse possession of land for the period of 10 years ending on the date of the application. For this purpose, the requirement of "adverse possession" was satisfied if a period of limitation under section 15 of the Limitation Act 1980 would have run in his favour in relation to the estate: 2002 Act, schedule 6 para. 11(1). An application under paragraph 1 of schedule 6 had to be accompanied by a statutory declaration setting out the evidence relied upon in support of the claim: Land Registration Rules 2003, rule 188. The fact that the period of adverse possession referred to in paragraph 1(1) of schedule 6 was 10 years, and not 12 years, was not intended to make it easier to acquire a possessory title.

To understand its impact, the reduction in the period has to be read with the other provisions of schedule 6.

86. Where a person applied to be registered under paragraph 1(1) of schedule 6, the registrar was obliged to notify the registered proprietor: schedule 6 para. 2(1). The registered proprietor was then entitled to require that the application be dealt with under schedule 6 para. 5. Under para. 5, the applicant was only entitled to be registered if any one of three conditions was met. The three conditions were restrictive. It was not enough for the applicant simply to show that he had been in adverse possession for 10 years. However, the second condition (in paragraph 5(3)) would apply to a case where the applicant had been in adverse possession for 12 years before 13 October 2003 and so, under the transitional provision in schedule 12 para 18(1), had retained an entitlement to be registered as proprietor. It is the practice of the Land Registry to require an application for registration on this ground to be made by the normal application form, AP1: the current Land Registry Practice Guide 5 (July 2013 edition) says so at para. 5.2. This was also the position under the March 2003 edition of the Practice Guide: see at para. 10.2.

87. Thus, under the new regime, a person is not entitled to be registered as proprietor just by being in adverse possession for a period of time. After 10 years of adverse possession, he may apply to be registered, but notice of his application is given to the registered proprietor who can block the application, save in the three special cases. However, the regime involves the registered proprietor taking action to block the application (by giving notice requiring that it be dealt with under para. 5). The corollary is that if the registered proprietor does not require the application to be dealt with under paragraph 5, then the applicant is entitled to be registered as the new proprietor of the estate: schedule 6 para. 4.

88. Although the registered proprietor can normally block an application made under paragraph 1(1) of schedule 6 by requiring it to be dealt with under paragraph 5, this does not mean that the matter is permanently dealt with by the application not succeeding at that point. This is because the person in adverse possession is entitled to make a further application for registration, this time under para. 6 of schedule 6. This requires him to show that he has been in adverse possession of the estate from the date of his application under para. 1(1) of schedule 6 until the last day of the period of 2 years beginning with the date of rejection of that application. If the applicant satisfies this requirement then he is entitled to be registered as the new proprietor of the estate: schedule 6 para. 7. The result is that following the rejection of the application under para. 1 of schedule 6, the registered proprietor must take action to recover possession of the land (or legitimise the possession of it) otherwise, after a further 2 years, the person in adverse possession will have an unanswerable claim to be registered on a second application.'

The 2016 Law Commission Consultation Paper, Law Commission CP 227

2–73 The Law Commission looked again at the reforms brought in by the Land Registration Act 2002 in its 2016 Consultation Paper (CP) 227: 'Updating the Land Registration Act 2002'. As well as a useful history of the reforms of adverse possession (2.44–2.45; 17.1–17.15) a number of proposals were put forward.[1] The consultation period closed on 30 June 2016, but at the date at which this supplement aims to state the law, the Law Commission had not published its recommendations following that consultation. The proposals made relevant to the law of adverse possession were as follows:

(1) Limiting the ability to rectify where there is a mistaken removal of the registered proprietor to ten years, to mirror the time limit under adverse possession, unless the new proprietor consents or contributed to the mistake by fraud or lack of proper care (13.121–13.126).
(2) Addressing the effect of *Parshall v Hackney* [2013] Ch 568 and its aftermath. The proposal is that, where double registration occurs so that, by accident, one piece of land has more than one registered title applicable to it, the matter should be dealt with by the proposed reforms to defeasibility rather than by adverse possession (13.133–13.151). By defeasibility is meant rectification and alteration of the register, which is to be overhauled (see Part 4 of the Law Commission CP in relation to that part of the proposed reforms).
(3) Providing a non-exhaustive list of factors which may be used to distinguish boundary and property disputes (15.11 and 15.30–15.36). The courts have held that, where there is a dispute about whether land is or is not included in a registered title, the dispute may be considered as falling into two different categories – a 'property' dispute and a 'boundary dispute': see para 33–06 in the Main Work, *Lee v Barrey* [1957] Ch 251, *Strachey v Ramage* [2008] 2 P&CR 8, and *Drake v Fripp* [2012] 1 P&CR 4. If the dispute is where the boundaries of a piece of land with registered title are, it is a 'boundary dispute', and if the court decides in favour of the registered proprietor, the order does not vest new land in him, but rather produces the result that the title plan shows the general boundary in a more accurate position than before. But if the dispute is whether a distinct piece of land is, or is not, owned by the registered proprietor, then it is a 'property dispute', and if it is decided in favour of the registered proprietor, he establishes title to a new piece of land, and does not simply correct the location of the boundaries of an existing piece of land.
(4) Part 6 (Chapter 17) of Law Commission CP 227 is dedicated to Adverse Possession.[2] The Law Commission are not proposing to overhaul the

---

1 C Harpum, architect of the original Land Registration Act 2002, has given a very detailed response to this paper, including the matters referred to below, which is available at http://www.falcon-chambers.com/images/uploads/articles/Response_to_LC_CP_227_on_Land_Registration_%282%29.pdf

2 With a useful review of the law at 17.9–17.15.

scheme under the 2002 Act. Instead, the proposals will simply review three aspects ((a)–(c) below) of the machinery for applications under Schedule 6 of that Act, and, secondly, four substantive areas of the law of adverse possession insofar as they interact with Schedule 6 (listed under (d) below). The proposals in summary are:

(a) That once a Schedule 6 application is rejected, a further application should only be made under the Schedule 6 paragraph 6 conditions (17.24). This spells out what is current Land Registration practice. It is hoped that it will be spelled out when an application has in fact been 'rejected' to avoid further creative argument. This is a very sensible proposal.

(b) The Schedule 6, paragraph 5 conditions where an objection is received requiring the application to be dealt with under paragraph 5 will be revisited, and consideration will be given to the removal of the first two conditions. This means that the ability of the Tribunal to resolve proprietary estoppel claims will be revisited, and consideration will be given to whether the second condition should be limited in scope to the classes of cases in which it is encountered, namely applications by squatters to be registered where they have successfully completed 12 years' adverse possession of the land while unregistered, which has subsequently become registered without their knowledge (17.25–17.35).

(c) The third condition will be re-evaluated, in particular in relation to the 'reasonable belief' test and the period for which such belief has to be held. Presently the statutory words have been heavily glossed by the cases (17.36–17.47).

(d) Clarification of the relationship between Schedule 6 of the 2002 Act and the law of adverse possession (17.48). Specifically:
    (i) Reform of the law relating to first registration of paper titles which have in fact been extinguished by adverse possession (17.49–17.62);
    (ii) Consideration of whether a squatter should be allowed to apply for first registration with possessory title before his 12 years are up and to clarify that the sole basis on which a squatter can acquire title to registered land is under the Schedule 6 process (17.63–17.71);
    (iii) Clarification of the law relating to squatters who have become registered by mistake before time has lapsed, to avoid the problems identified by Judge Rhys in *Moore v Buxton* REF/ 2007/1216 (17.72–17.79);
    (iv) To address the muddled law relating to encroachments by tenants, though it is proposed to look only at encroachments on third party land (17.80–17.86). Encroachments against the landlord by his own tenant are to be excluded (17.87–17.88).

Chapter 3

Interpretation, policy and human rights

3–08 In *Parshall v Hackney* [2013] Ch 568, the Court of Appeal considered the broad policy relationship between land registration on the one hand, and limitation on the other, at [19]–[25]. In particular, the Court of Appeal endorsed the view expressed in Megarry and Wade's *Law of Real Property* (8th edn, Sweet and Maxwell, 2012), [35–070] that the modern law, following on from the Land Registration Act 2002, is that adverse possession now no longer bars title to registered land, and the limitation periods are expressly disapplied by s 96 of that Act.

3–48 In *Baxter v Mannion* [2011] EWCA Civ 120, the Court of Appeal upheld the decision of Henderson J below. Where a person was registered as proprietor of land on the basis of his claim to title by adverse possession, the register could be altered to delete that registration if it was subsequently proved that he had not been in adverse possession and so should never have been registered. This was a 'mistake' in the register, which the registrar had power to correct. Henderson J considered that it would be a breach of A1P1 of the ECHR if the Land Registration Act 2002 could not correct such a fundamental error and the Court of Appeal (at [34]) agreed with him.

Human Rights Defences

3–59 It is to be noted that private individuals cannot set up human rights arguments in claims brought by other private individuals simply because the court is itself a 'public authority'. Certain *obiter dicta* of the Supreme Court, in *Manchester City Council v Pinnock* [2011] UKSC 6 (at [50]) and the Court of Appeal in *Malik v Fassenfelt* [2013] EWCA Civ 798 appeared to have left open the prospect of purely horizontal human rights defences against possession claims based on that argument.[1] However, it is considered that this door has been firmly shut by the Supreme Court in *McDonald v McDonald* [2016] UKSC 28, at [40] and following.[2] The Supreme Court held that the court is 'merely the forum for the determination of the civil right in dispute between the parties.'

1 By which we mean defences suggesting that the Claimant is breaching the Defendant's human rights, and not that the court (in exercising a discretion, for example) or Parliament (in enacting legislation of failing to take steps to safeguard the Defendant's human rights) are doing so.

2 *Couper v Albion Properties Limited* [2014] EWHC 265 (Ch) is a further unusual instance of a human rights argument being deployed, this time at the enforcement stage of possession proceedings. The underlying proceedings are *Couper v Albion Properties Limited* [2013] EWHC 2993 (Ch).

Chapter 4
Title to land

4–17 See too *Prashar v Tunbridge Wells BC* [2012] EWHC 1734 (Ch).

Chapter 5

The significance of adverse possession, discontinuance and dispossession

5–17 The relationship between dispossession and discontinuance was further considered in *Norbrook Laboratories v Maguire* [2012] NICh 32, especially at [45].

Chapter 6

The requirement that possession must be 'adverse' and continuous

6–14 The statement expressed in this paragraph of the Main Work, that '*possession of land is only adverse as against the owner, if the owner of that land is entitled to recover possession from that person*', was referred to in *Parshall v Hackney* [2013] Ch 568 at [40].

6–16 Further statements of the principle that (apart from the special cases of deemed adverse possession) lawful possession is not 'adverse' are to be found in the decisions of the Divisional Court in *R (on the application of Heaton) v HM Land Registry* [2013] EWHC 2449 (Admin) at [15]; the First-tier Tribunal in *Openshaw v P&F Properties Limited* REF/2013/0222 at [26]; in the Court of Appeal in *Smart v Lambeth LBC* [2013] EWCA Civ 1375 at [32]; see also *Belford v Glass* [2014] NIQB 134.

6–30 Add (7): Accidental registration.

Accidental Registration

6–47A In *Parshall v Hackney* [2013] Ch 568, an unusual situation arose. P had acquired land which had, for many years, included within its paper title and registered title (registered since 1904), a triangle of land suitable for parking a car. H was the owner of neighbouring land, first registered in 1980. The Land Registry mistakenly included the triangle in that latter title too. Then, in 2000, the Land Registry computerised its plans. In the course of so doing, the triangle was removed from P's title, where it in fact belonged, and included in H's registered title. On spotting the error, P applied to have H's title rectified, and H resisted on the grounds of limitation. H argued that there had been adverse possession for 12 years from 1988, when H claimed to have taken possession. During that period, therefore, both P and H had separate and concurrent registered titles to the disputed land.

6–47B The issue for the Court of Appeal was therefore whether to prefer P's paper title claim (based on prior registration, wrongfully altered by the Land Registry in 2000) or H's possessory title claim. The Court of Appeal determined that H could not be in adverse possession as a matter of law, as H had, at all material times during the period of possession, been the registered proprietor of the land in question ([87]). There was, therefore, no dispossession under the Limitation Act 1980 (which governed the position at the time). Furthermore, due to the concurrent registration, P did not in fact have a claim for the recovery of land which could trigger the running of the limitation period: see at [88]–[90]. P's cause of action was a claim to have a mistake rectified, which was not subject to a statutory limitation period and which was a necessary antecedent to P having a claim for the recovery of land. The suggestion that there is no accrued cause of action to recover land where the putative claimant must first rectify another's title to vest a claim for possession seems contrary to *Ramzan v Brookwide* [2011] EWCA Civ 985.

6–47C The above might be thought to give rise to an issue about the operation of the general boundaries rule (Main Work, paras 33–04 to 33–05). It is often the case that the Land Registry plan does not correspond with the true extent of the underlying paper title and admissible evidence for construction. If a paper title owner has secured a more generous registered boundary line, does that mean that the paper title owner has deprived himself of the ability to claim adverse possession from that point in time by reason of his more expansive registered title? The Court of Appeal dealt with that point briefly at [96]:

> 'In my judgment, the general boundaries rule does not help the respondent for the simple reason that the dispute in this case is not a dispute about the position or delineation of the boundaries of No 29 or No 31. The dispute is about title to registered land (the disputed land.) The question is who has the better title to the disputed land. It is not about where the boundary should be drawn as between No 29 and No 31.'

6–47D A similar distinction is drawn in the recent authorities on boundary agreements, where the courts distinguish between agreements to dispose of land on the one hand, and agreements to clarify a boundary on the other. However, it is difficult to draw the line between a 'boundary' and 'title to land' case in practice, which may be illustrated by comparing *Drake v Fripp* [2011] EWCA Civ 1279 (a boundary clarification case) and *Parshall.* It is also difficult to see how this fits with the earlier Court of Appeal decision in *IAM Group v Chowdery* [2012] EWCA Civ 505 – in that case, the squatter succeeded because he reasonably believed that a room above a flat adjacent to his own was within his title and hence subject to the general boundaries rule.

6–47E The law is presently as it stands in *Parshall.* However, it is suggested that in two respects the Court of Appeal's conclusions may be open to doubt:

(1) Its treatment of the general boundaries rule, the scope of which is presently open to some considerable doubt; and
(2) The question of whether the analysis that a true owner, unable to constitute a possession claim based on paper title because of the need to rectify first can truly be said not to have a right to recover land, so that time does not run.

6–47F The Law Commission is proposing to review the effects of *Parshall*: see 2–73(2) and (3) above.

6–52 Add footnote after colon: this was applied in *Waters v Evans* REF/2016/0936 (Judge Michael Michell).

6–55 Add to Fn 3: see discussion of this case in *Bezkorowajny v Dawson* REF/2010/1203; 2011/0521.

Chapter 7
The meaning of 'possession'

7–17 Fn 36 add: endorsed and restated by the Privy Council in *Armbrister v Lightbourn* [2012] UKPC 40, at [82].

7–23 Naturally, however, the more third party rights are exercisable over a given piece of land, the more difficult it might become in practice to take effective control over it. This may be because the land in question, for instance highways, makes such conduct illegal (as to which see paragraph 7–130 of the Main Work and this Update). It may also separately be that the land in question is constantly in use so that control is not a practical possibility, which may have been the issue in *Mellstrom v Badgworthy Land Company Limited* REF/2008/1498, 2009/0290, 2009/0953. See too Chapter 12 of the Main work.

Fn 50 add: So, for instance, the existence of a commons scheme is not fatal to an adverse possession claim, provided that adverse possession is established on the facts: *Mellstrom v Badgworthy Land Company Limited* REF/2008/1498, 2009/0290, 2009/0953.

7–25 This passage in the Main Work has been described as 'remarkable' by Judge Michael Mark in *Port of London v Mendoza* REF/2011/0751 at [57]:

> 'In his skeleton argument, [Counsel for the Respondent] contended that a squatter could not establish possession unless and until he had effective control of the land. He appears to have relied on a passage in *Jourdan and Radley-Gardner on Adverse Possession* (2011 ed) at paragraphs 7–25 to 7–26 to the effect that there must first be conduct amounting to acquiescence on the part of the true owner. This is a somewhat remarkable passage when the true owner often cannot be found and the point has been abandoned by Mr Stonor in his closing submissions.'

Counsel reserved his position on acquiescence on appeal (the fate of which is unknown). The passage in question is based on a number of cases (summarised in the following paragraphs in the Main Work) that establish that for control to be effective, the paper title owner must either be aware of the squatter's attempt to take control of the land and do nothing to prevent it, or that the paper title owner is ignorant of what is happening.

7–29 Add footnote following colon: see also *Wakolo v DPP* [2012] EWHC 611 (Admin).

Must the Land Being Claimed Be Capable of Definition

7–32A In *Balevents Ltd v Sartori* [2014] EWHC 1164 (Ch), the squatter failed because the use was sporadic and over a shifting area. The squatter therefore failed principally because exclusive possession could not be shown; however Morgan J also pointed out that the fact that the use was not always in the same location meant that no adverse possession could be demonstrated on the facts. There is perhaps a parallel here with the law of prescription, where the extent of the right acquired will depend on the land which has been used (as held in *Lynn Shellfish Ltd v Loose* [2016] UKSC 14). It will, therefore, not be possible to make out an adverse possession claim if the squatter's use was not always in the same location (unless he can invoke the principles set out in Chapters 10 and 11 of the Main Work as updated below).

7–32B This is supported by *Thomas W Ward Ltd v Alexander Bruce (Grays) Ltd* [1959] 2 Lloyds Rep 472[1], where it was stated at page 478 that:

> 'In order to acquire a title by adverse possession under the Limitation Act 1939, it seems to us to at least be necessary that the claimants should be able to define the area adversely possessed by them. In the present case, the area has extended and may, by the action of the tide, or indeed of the appellants', be curtailed, and it seems to us that there is no room here for this claim. It is to be observed that it never occurred to the appellants at the outset to make such a claim. They relied solely upon the acquisition of an easement, and it was not until after considering for some time the respondents' contention, that the claim preferred could not be supported as an easement at all, that the alternative claim was added as an afterthought.'

7–32C The issue was further considered by Mann J in *Port of London Authority v Tower Bridge Yacht and Boat Company Ltd* [2013] EWHC 3084 (Ch), where he stated at:

> '273. The first is a general reason which is more procedural than substantive. The defendant claims a limitation title to very small defined areas. Yet it has not proved where those areas are, with sufficient clarity for these purposes. Someone claiming a possessory title (as I shall call it, for the sake of convenience) should be able to point to the physical extent of the land to which possession is claimed. The defendant cannot do that. All it can do is to point to approximate positions in which a root can be found (save for two roots where the position is apparent). The position is approximate because it is not possible (or, if possible, it has not been done) to define precisely where the roots are. Mr Honey could not do it, and (as I have observed before in this judgment) all the previous charts and plans probably do no more than show

1 And see first instance decision in *Port of London v Mendoza* REF/2011/0751 at [47] and following, there (relying on *Bawtree v Levett-Scrivener* REF/2005/1730 pointing out that complete clarity of the boundary is not the test either. *Franklin v Smith* [2015] UKFTT 0048 (PC).

where chains go into the mud (or water), not where the roots are. Furthermore, even if the position could be shown, the physical extent of the space cannot be identified. The root may be stones of various shapes; or a concrete block; or an engine block; or an oddly shaped piece of wood; or something which has decayed over time so that it now has a different shape. In the case of the new roots it is the shape of an anchor, but that shape has not been specified. While resolving some of these uncertainties might just about make it appropriate to make a finding (or register a title) in terms which achieve sufficient clarity and certainty (as to which I make no determination), cumulatively they present a picture in which the position and extent of the land claimed has not been proved sufficiently.

274. This is not the same point as that taken by Mr Harpum and referred to above, namely that Mr Lacey cannot intend to possess something he does not know the position of. The point in the case relied on (*Thomas Ward v Bruce*) is a different one. It appears in that case that the area of land to which title was claimed varied according to the state of the business (shipbreaking) and the nature and scope of the work being done from time to time. At page 478 Harman LJ said:

> "In order to acquire [a]title by adverse possession and any Limitation Act 1939, it seems to us at least necessary that the claimants should be able to define the area adversely possessed by them. In the present case, the area has extended and may, by the action of the tide, or, indeed, of the appellants', be curtailed, and it seems to us that there is no room here for this claim."

That is an observation about the inability to define the scope of the land affected by the claim because it varied from time to time. That is not the point in the present case. In theory, and with enough effort, the position occupied by each block and anchor could be ascertained. The fact that Mr Lacey may not know at the moment precisely where each one is, and the physical shape of it, is not a substantive part of the claim. The position and shape are what they are, and do not fluctuate as apparently the area involved in *Thomas Ward v Bruce*. The point that I make is a more procedural one. As a matter of procedure and description, if you cannot point out what land you are claiming adverse possession of, you cannot get a declaration that you are entitled to anything in particular. If the problem of the identification of the space occupied by each mooning feature were fixed, then this problem would go away.'

7–32D Of course, it will frequently be possible to establish with certainty what the land is over which possession has been enjoyed, and a claim to too much land will not mean that the claim to the lesser land truly claimed will fail: *Frankland v Smith* [2015] UKFTT 0048 (PC) and the discussion in *Port of London Authority v Paul Mendoza* [2016] EWLandRA 2011_0751 at first instance. However if the use has in fact been over a shifting area over time, then the claim will fail because the squatter will not have been in adverse possession of any land for the full period of time unless he can bring himself under the rules considered in Chapters 10 and 11 of the Main Work.

7–38 An example of the user/possession distinction in practice may be found in *Port of London Authority v Tower Bridge Yacht and Boat Company Ltd* [2013] EWHC 3084 (Ch), where the position in relation to mooring was considered. Mann J (at [273] and following) decided that, whilst it was possible to be in exclusive possession of a small piece of land, on the facts of the case before him, the correct analysis was that this was mere limited user of a larger piece of land.

7–44 This paragraph was applied in *U Po Chu v Tsang Pui Ling* (DCMP 467 of 2013).

7–48 For a 'shifting population' case, concerning members of a cricket club, where the use was held have been with the consent of the owner, see *Openshaw v P&F Properties Limited* REF/2013/0222. In his judgment, Judge Timothy Cowen expressed the view that, on a claim to adverse possession under Sch 6 to the Land Registration Act 2002 by members of a club, the shifting membership body of the club as a whole was not capable of having been in single exclusive possession, and nor could the successive groups which made up the membership claim to be 'successors in title' for the purposes of Sch 6, para 11. This seems questionable. If the members of an unincorporated association such as a sports club carry on activities which would constitute possession if the association was incorporated, it could be regarded as unsatisfactory that the absence of the legal fiction of a corporate person should prevent them from being in possession. See also the article by Dr. Alan Dowling, 'Adverse Possession and Unincorporated Associations' (2003) 54.3 Northern Ireland Legal Quarterly, 272 and *Carcillo v The Great Western Allotment Association* REF/2014/0354.

7–55 It is clear that the fact that a third party might have some pre-existing rights to the land does not prevent a squatter from taking possession of the land, though he will do so subject to those rights: *Mellstrom v Badgworthy Land Company Limited* REF/2008/1498, 2009/0290, 2009/0953. In *Akram v Stott* REF/2013/1088, temporary fencing by a third party was held to be irrelevant.

7–76A The issue of concurrent use was also considered in *Zarb v Parry* [2011] EWCA Civ 1306, [83]. The paper title owner had undertaken works which were preparatory to the re-taking of possession – including erection of fence posts (without installing the fence) and taking measurements. It was argued that these 'mere entries', though not of themselves amounting to a factual re-taking of possession, were enough to stop time running. The cases referred to in Chapter 7 of the Main Work were not considered by the Court of Appeal, but support its conclusions at [43]:[1]

1 See also paragraph [57].

'The facts in *Bligh v Martin* were very different from those of the present case. This appeal is concerned with part of a garden, not farmland. Pennycuick J did not have to consider the effect of an attempt to retake possession that had been thwarted by the adverse possessor, or abandoned. Nor did he have to consider the effect of an oral declaration of intent by the paper title owner communicated to the adverse possessor. In my judgment, however, the principle on which *Bligh* was decided, namely that the factual possession of the adverse possessor must be brought to an end is clearly correct and determines the result on this issue. The principle achieves a simple test for ascertaining whether the period of adverse possession has been brought to an end. Interruption will be overt and so it can be more easily proved or disproved if the question has to be litigated many years later. Furthermore, if the paper title owner did something less than exclude the adverse possessor, such as plant a flag, put up a notice or make an oral declaration of ownership, the adverse possessor would continue to have factual possession in the sense defined in *Pye*. A person might, therefore, continue to have the intent to possess and factual possession throughout the period of any interruption of his adverse possession by symbolic acts such as I have mentioned. It would, in my judgment, be inconsistent with *Pye* if an adverse possessor could at one and the same time fulfil the requirements for adverse possession but yet have his possession effectively interrupted by the paper title owner. Finally, there is no need for the paper title owner to know that he is bringing the adverse possession to an end or to say that he is doing so: it is the quality of the acts which matters and not any oral declarations.'

7–76B It is considered that the true position is as follows:[1]

(1) If there is concurrent use throughout the period under consideration between the paper title owner and the putative squatter, then the latter will not be able to claim adverse possession. This is either because the latter will never have been exclusive possession, or because there will never have been acquiescence in the sense set out in paragraphs 7–25ff and following of the Main Work.
(2) If, however, there is a moment in time at which the squatter takes exclusive possession of the land, then subsequent concurrent use by the paper title owner falling short of re-taking possession by the latter (ie a true 'interruption') will not stop time running.
(3) What is required where adverse possession has crystallised, is either an action to recover land with enforcement of the possession order,[2] or factual recovery of possession of the land.
(4) It is clear from the cases that concurrent exercise by third parties of limited rights (or activities which could be attributable to limited rights) will not preclude a squatter from being in adverse possession, unless it can be said that such concurrent use results in the squatter not having exclusive control.

1 And see the discussion in *Calhaem v Gentil* [2016] EWLandRA 2015_0272 (Judge Michell).
2 *Grand Wayfair Investment Company Limited v Chan Yung Kan* [2014] HKCA 481.

7-88A In *Zarb v Parry* [2011] EWCA Civ 1306, one of the questions was whether the paper owner had re-taken possession of a strip of land. The acts were quite limited, involving some measurements and excavation of fences, which works were then abandoned. Arden LJ considered *Bligh v Martin* and stated the position in relation to that as follows:

> '[39] The paper title owner has the advantage in law that, to effect repossession of property, it is sufficient to show that possession has been resumed for short period of time. This was established in *Randall v Stevens* (1853) 2 E & B 641, 118 ER 907 where a landlord evicted a tenant who had failed to pay any rent for twenty years. Statute provided that a house could not be repossessed simply by exercising a right of entry. Lord Campbell LC, giving the judgment of the Court of Queen's Bench on appeal from a judgment given at assizes, held that entry could be made "by stepping on any corner of the land in the night time and pronouncing a few words, without any intention or wish to take possession." However, where possession was taken with an intention to possess, then "whether possession was retained by the landlord an hour or a week must for this purpose [i.e. taking possession other than by mere entry] be immaterial."
>
> [40] The adverse possessor is, therefore, at risk of losing possession for a brief period of time, perhaps while he is out taking a walk or doing some shopping. The fact that the paper title owner can interrupt his possession in this way lends support to the view that the act of interruption should be effective to bring the adverse possessor's exclusive possession to an end. It would potentially be unfair if a paper title owner could interrupt adverse possession by the simple act of erecting a notice on the property saying, for example, "Private Property – Keep Out", so that the period of adverse possession will start all over again.
>
> [...]
>
> [42] The facts in *Bligh v Martin* were very different from those of the present case. This appeal is concerned with part of a garden, not farmland. Pennycuick J did not have to consider the effect of an attempt to retake possession that had been thwarted by the adverse possessor, or abandoned. Nor did he have to consider the effect of an oral declaration of intent by the paper title owner communicated to the adverse possessor. In my judgment, however, the principle on which *Bligh* was decided, namely that the factual possession of the adverse possessor must be brought to an end is clearly correct and determines the result on this issue. The principle achieves a simple test for ascertaining whether the period of adverse possession has been brought to an end. Interruption will be overt and so it can be more easily proved or disproved if the question has to be litigated many years later. Furthermore, if the paper title owner did something less than exclude the adverse possessor, such as plant a flag, put up a notice or make an oral declaration of ownership, the adverse possessor would continue to have factual possession in the sense

defined in *Pye*. A person might, therefore, continue to have the intent to possess and factual possession throughout the period of any interruption of his adverse possession by symbolic acts such as I have mentioned. It would, in my judgment, be inconsistent with *Pye* if an adverse possessor could at one and the same time fulfil the requirements for adverse possession but yet have his possession effectively interrupted by the paper title owner. Finally, there is no need for the paper title owner to know that he is bringing the adverse possession to an end or to say that he is doing so: it is the quality of the acts which matters and not any oral declarations.'

7–88B She concluded (at [44]) that '*It was not enough that the Zarbs planted stakes or took other steps symbolic of taking possession of the whole of the Strip.*' The Master of the Rolls found greater difficulty with the point, and gave more detailed reasons, though in agreement with Arden LJ. He stated as follows:

'[67] I turn to the Zarbs' second argument, which is that the Parrys' adverse possession of the strip was interrupted in July 2007, when, it is said, the Zarbs re-took possession of the strip. On the facts of this case, such an interruption would be fatal to the Parrys' claim to have title by adverse possession even though they had clocked up more than ten, and even more than twelve, years adverse possession by that time – see section 98(1) of, para 5(4)(c) of schedule 1, and para 1(2) of schedule 6, to the 2002 Act.

[68] The evidence on this point is set out in full in para 7 above. Although the Zarbs were present on the strip for less than an hour, they carried out acts which may be said to be to be (i) inherently redolent of ownership, and/or (ii) signalling the retaking of possession. Chopping down the elderflower tree is in category (i). Category (ii) includes Mr Zarb marking off the paper boundary with a tape, stating that he was taking back the strip as it belonged to him, and refusing to vacate until threatened with the police being called. Into both categories are uprooting the Parrys' fence and banging in posts to mark the paper boundary.

[69] The fact that the Zarbs were present on the strip for less than an hour does not prevent their actions when on the strip from being a retaking of possession – see *Randall v Stevens* (1853) 2 E&B 641, per Lord Campbell CJ. In that case, it was held that possession had been retaken, but the facts were stronger than in this case in that the paper title-holder physically evicted the occupier, his family and all his furniture, albeit only for an hour, from the property in question, which was a house. Accordingly, there is no doubt that the person claiming adverse possession was physically completely excluded from the property, which remained, albeit for a short period, in the exclusive occupation and control of the paper title owner.

[70] The judgment of Erle CJ in *Allen v England* (1862) 3 F&F 49, at any rate at first sight, gives some support for the Zarbs' case

in that it includes the proposition that "every time [the paper title owner] puts his foot on the land, it [is] in his possession". However, that apparently rather extreme view is in my judgment explained by reference to the particular facts of the case, which involved "permissive use of a garden", as Pennycuick J put it in *Bligh v Martin* [1968] 1 WLR 804. In that later case, it was found that, although he had occupied and made use of the land in question, the paper title owner had never retaken possession of it. However, just as the facts in *Randall* 2 E&B 641, and indeed in *Allen* 3 F&F 52, were more strongly in favour of the paper title owner than those of this case, so it seems to me clear that the facts in *Bligh* [1968] 1 WLR 804 were weaker rom the point of view of the paper title owner than those in the present case.

[71] However, the decision in *Bligh* [1968] 1 WLR 804 is valuable for present purposes in that Pennycuick J gave some guidance of general application, when he said that "in the ordinary case of adverse possession ... one must find that the [paper title] owner took possession in the ordinary sense of that word, to the exclusion of the [person claiming adverse possession]". Given the fact-specific and nebulous nature of possession, I consider that, in so far as general guidance can be given in relation to the task of deciding whether, on particular facts, the paper title owner has retaken possession at any time during the period of alleged adverse possession, that is probably as good as it can get.

[72] In the present case, applying that general guidance, I have reached the conclusion that the Zarbs did not retake possession of the strip on the occasion in July 2007 described in para 7 above, and that the judge was entitled to reach that conclusion (which he did in very brief terms). What the Zarbs did, in my opinion, was to prepare to take possession, but they never completed the exercise. When they knew the Parrys were away from their property on a shopping expedition, the Zarbs took preliminary steps with a view to excluding the Parrys from the strip, by removing some of the Parrys' fence, and starting to erect their own fence (presumably on the paper boundary), but they got no further than taking preliminary steps. When the confrontation with the Parrys occurred, the strip had not been fenced off from the Parrys' property by the Zarbs, and, although the Zarbs initially threatened to exclude the Parrys when challenged and asked to vacate, the Zarbs ultimately backed down, and departed from the strip, leaving the Parrys in control.

[73] In other words, while the Zarbs embarked on an enterprise which, if it had been completed, would have involved their retaking possession of the strip, they were interrupted by the Parrys before the enterprise had been completed, and, in the ensuing confrontation, they abandoned the enterprise. Accordingly, rather than retaking possession of the strip, it seems to me that, although they got some way towards achieving that aim, the Zarbs were thwarted in their attempt to do so, and had not

completed it before the Parrys appeared, and, thereafter, when challenged, the Zarbs backed down pretty promptly (and, most people would I think say, properly).

[74] Unlike the adverse possessors of the house in *Randall* 2 E&B 641, the Parrys never lost control or possession of the strip to the paper title owners, although it may have been a pretty close run thing: if they had stayed out shopping for another hour, the Zarbs may have completed the execution of their plan. However, as Pennycuick J pointed out in *Bligh* 812, in order to succeed in their argument, the Zarbs would have to have taken possession "to the exclusion of the [Parrys]".

[75] It is true that the Zarbs also did things which may arguably be characterised as acts of ownership in the form of chopping down a tree and pulling up a fence, and they must be taken into account as part of the totality of the facts of that rather fraught hour on 29 July 2007. However, even taking them into account, I do not consider that the Zarbs did enough to be able to say that they effectively excluded the Parrys from the strip. The pulling up of the fence was part of the preparatory work done in order to retake possession, but, as I have said, that work never reached fruition. As for the tree-chopping, it seems to have been little more than a rather spiteful act involving an elder, which many people would characterise as a shrub rather than a tree. Further, although the Zarbs' case cannot fail simply because of the fact that they are relying on events which took place over a very short period, I do consider that, when assessing whether the Parrys were excluded, the fact that the Zarbs rely on events which occurred over a very short length of time is a relevant factor.'

7–99 Add to Fn 203: *McCann v McCann* [2013] NICh 7.

7–127 Add to Fn 262: *Mills v Rapley* REF/2014/0317.

The Evolution of the Ex Turpi Causa Defence[1]

7–130A The Supreme Court has now considered the question of illegality and its bearing on private law actions in a series of cases. The origin of the illegality defence may be traced to Lord Mansfield in *Holman v Johnson* (1775) 1 Cowp 341, 343, where he stated that '*No court will lend its aid to a man who founds his cause of action upon an immoral or an illegal act*.' He went on to explain that the rule was one of public policy:

'If, from the plaintiff's own stating or otherwise, the cause of action appears to arise ex turpi causa, or the transgression of a positive law of this country, there the court says he has no right to be assisted. It

1 What follows is a consideration of the defence in the context of non-contractual claims. In contractual claims, the operation of the defence might be different, although the Supreme Court appears to treat the defence as being the same in all private law claim contexts.

is upon that ground the court goes; not for the sake of the defendant, but because they will not lend their aid to such a plaintiff. So if the plaintiff and defendant were to change sides, and the defendant was to bring his action against the plaintiff, the latter would then have the advantage of it; for where both are equally in fault, potiorest conditio defendentis.'

7–130B The tension in the cases is between two general approaches to the illegality question:

(1) Should the defence be based strongly on causation, so that a claim must fail if it can be shown that it cannot be made out without reliance on relevant turpitude? The benefit of that rule is a degree of mechanical certainty. The problem with that rule is that it leads to arbitrary results, depending on whether turpitude can be avoided by skilled pleading or by the fortuitous availability of rules of law not dependent upon the turpitude.
(2) Should the court instead look at the underlying policies to determine whether the defence is engaged, so that, even if the claim necessarily involves a degree of reliance on turpitude of a relevant kind, that is not automatically a bar to a successful claim?

7–130C The courts initially applied a very open-textured 'public conscience' approach to the defence, which brought with the merits of flexibility the usual vice of uncertainty. This approach was disavowed in the House of Lords by the majority in *Tinsley v Milligan* [1994] 1 AC 340. The facts of that case were that the parties had arranged for property to be purchased and held in the sole name of one of them, so that the other could make a fraudulent benefits claim. The non-owning party then wished to reclaim her share of the property when their relationship ended. The majority decided that she succeeded on the grounds of resulting trust, and that this basis of claim did not need to rely on any illegality as it operated independently from it. The non-owning party would, however, have failed had their relationship been one to which the presumption of advancement applied.[1] Lord Browne-Wilkinson noted the arbitrary difference in result, which he explained on the basis that illegality was a procedural bar to advancing a claim, as opposed to a substantive part of the law. The majority decision has been the subject of criticism, including by the Law Commission,[2] and one can discern in later cases, including *Bakewell Management Ltd v Brandwood* [2004] 2 AC 519 (a case concerning prescription and easements) and *Gray v Thames Trains Ltd* [2009] AC 1339 (a case concerning personal injury damages), a departure from that mechanical approach. Those cases appear to stand for the wider proposition that a claim based on relevant turpitude might be allowed provided that the claim did not run counter to the policy of the rule infringed.

1 *Collier v Collier* [2002] EWCA 1095 illustrates that arbitrariness.
2 The Illegality Defence: A Consultative Report (LCCP 189); followed by the 2010 Report, The Illegality Defence (Law Com 320).

7–130D This mechanical and arbitrary operation of the defence led to the softening of that test in *Stone & Rolls Ltd v Moore Stephens* [2009] 1 AC 1391. The approach in *Stone & Rolls* was more open textured, with Lord Phillips of Worth Matravers (at paragraph 25]) stating as follows:

> 'I do not believe… that it is right to proceed on the basis that the reliance test can automatically be applied as a rule of thumb. It is necessary to give consideration to the policy underlying ex turpi causa in order to decide whether this defence is bound to defeat [[the company's] claim.'

7–130E Accordingly, the mere fact that illegality formed part of the facts needed to be pleaded to constitute the cause of action was no longer sufficient to bar a claim as founded on illegality. It further had to be considered whether the need to rely on illegal conduct engaged the policy considerations underlying that principle. This point fell to be decided by the Supreme Court in *Hounga v Allen* [2014] UKSC 47 (concerning breach of employment law where the claimant was not allowed to work legally). Lord Wilson considered it most helpful to ask questions to ascertain whether the turpitude in that case was relevant to her claim in tort (paragraph 42]):

> '[i]t is necessary, first, to ask What is the aspect of public policy which founds the defence? and, second, to ask but is there another aspect of public policy to which application of the defence would run counter? […] The basis of this power, as I see it, lies in [[the] duty of the courts to preserve the integrity of the legal system, and is exercisable only where this concern is in issue. This concern is in issue where a damages] award in a civil suit would, in effect, allow a person to profit from illegal or wrongful conduct, or would permit an evasion or rebate of a penalty prescribed by the criminal law. The idea common to these instances is that the law refuses to give by its right hand what it takes away by its left hand.'

7–130F The law was then thrown into a degree of confusion by the later Supreme Court decision in *Les Laboratoires Servier & Anor v Apotex Inc* [2014] UKSC 55. *Hounga* was not referred to extensively in that judgment, which principally concerned the question of whether merely unlawful conduct – as opposed to illegal or *quasi*-criminal conduct (as explained in the judgment of Lord Sumption at [23]–[29]), engaged the *ex turpi cause* defence. This was decisively rejected by the Supreme Court. The judgment of Lord Sumption for the majority (at [19]–[20]) can, however, be read as following the *Tinsley* approach to illegality, without taking into account the change in approach which formed the basis of the *Hounga* decision. Despite the authority of the statement, the *Les Laboratories Servier* analysis was *obiter* given that the Supreme Court decided that there was no turpitude of the appropriate character to engage the illegality defence in the first place.

7–130G *Hounga* was, however, preferred by Sales LJ in *Best v Chief Land Registrar* [2015] EWCA Civ 17 (a case concerned with the illegality defence in the adverse possession context, of which more below), and was applied *Hniazdzilau v Vajgel* [2016] EWHC 15 (Ch).

7–130H The tension was resolved in *Patel v Mirza* [2016] UKSC 42. The majority judgment was that of Lord Toulson, with whom four other members of the panel agreed.[1] Mr Patel provided Mr Mirza with money so that Mr Mirza could invest it, using insider information. The arrangement amounted to a criminal conspiracy. Mr Mirza did not in fact invest the money, and did not pay it back either. Reviewing the cases, Lord Toulson favoured a more open-textured approach informed by *Hounga*:

> '[99] Looking behind the maxims, there are two broad discernible policy reasons for the common law doctrine of illegality as a defence to a civil claim. One is that a person should not be allowed to profit from his own wrongdoing. The other, linked, consideration is that the law should be coherent and not self-defeating, condoning illegality by giving with the left hand what it takes with the right hand.
>
> […]
>
> [101] So how is the court to determine the matter if not by some mechanistic process? In answer to that question I would say that one cannot judge whether allowing a claim which is in some way tainted by illegality would be contrary to the public interest, because it would be harmful to the integrity of the legal system, without a) considering the underlying purpose of the prohibition which has been transgressed, b) considering conversely any other relevant public policies which may be rendered ineffective or less effective by denial of the claim, and c) keeping in mind the possibility of overkill unless the law is applied with a due sense of proportionality. We are, after all, in the area of public policy. That trio of necessary considerations can be found in the case law.
>
> [121] The essential rationale of the illegality doctrine is that it would be contrary to the public interest to enforce a claim if to do so would be harmful to the integrity of the legal system (or, possibly, certain aspects of public morality, the boundaries of which have never been made entirely clear and which do not arise for consideration in this case). In assessing whether the public interest would be harmed in that way, it is necessary a) to consider the underlying purpose of the prohibition which has been transgressed and whether that purpose will be enhanced by denial of the claim, b) to consider any other relevant public policy on which the denial of the claim may have an impact and c) to consider whether denial of the claim would be a proportionate response to the illegality, bearing in mind that punishment is a

1 Lord Neuberger expressed himself to be in general agreement with the overall multi-factorial approach adopted by Lord Toulson. The minority – Lords Clark, Mance and Sumption, preferred the reliance test and regarded the multi-factorial approach as too vague.

matter for the criminal courts. Within that framework, various factors may be relevant, but it would be a mistake to suggest that the court is free to decide a case in an undisciplined way. The public interest is best served by a principled and transparent assessment of the considerations identified, rather by than the application of a formal approach capable of producing results which may appear arbitrary, unjust or disproportionate.'

Best

7–130I *Best v Chief Land Registrar* [2015] EWCA Civ 17 was decided after *Hounga* and *Les Laboratoires Servier*, but before *Patel*. The Supreme Court majority in *Patel* endorsed Sales LJ's judgment as exemplifying the majority approach and as correctly applying the *Hounga* approach (see *Patel* at [78], [79] and [103]). *Best* concerned the application of the recent offence of criminal squatting in residential property and its impact on adverse possession. The offence was introduced by s 144 of the Legal Aid, Sentencing and Punishment of Offenders Act 2012 (LASPOA). It provides as follows:

'(1) A person commits an offence if—
  (a) the person is in a residential building as a trespasser having entered it as a trespasser,
  (b) the person knows or ought to know that he or she is a trespasser, and
  (c) the person is living in the building or intends to live there for any period.
(2) The offence is not committed by a person holding over after the end of a lease or licence (even if the person leaves and re-enters the building).
(3) For the purposes of this section—
  (a) "building" includes any structure or part of a structure (including a temporary or moveable structure), and
  (b) a building is "residential" if it is designed or adapted, before the time of entry, for use as a place to live.
(4) For the purposes of this section the fact that a person derives title from a trespasser, or has the permission of a trespasser, does not prevent the person from being a trespasser.
(5) A person convicted of an offence under this section is liable on summary conviction to imprisonment for a term not exceeding 51 weeks or a fine not exceeding level 5 on the standard scale (or both).
(6) In relation to an offence committed before the commencement of section 281(5) of the Criminal Justice Act 2003, the reference in subsection (5) to 51 weeks is to be read as a reference to 6 months.
(7) For the purposes of subsection (1)(a) it is irrelevant whether the person entered the building as a trespasser before or after the commencement of this section'.

7–130J Sales LJ correctly identified *Hounga* as the correct statement of the relevant principles. He further rejected a broad submission by the respondent squatter to the effect that illegality could play no role in adverse possession at all.[1] Instead, he preferred the 'narrower' principle, that illegality had some role to play in Sch 6, para 1 but only in line with what was decided in *Hounga*. The *Hounga* principles were then applied to s 144 which then operated as follows:

> '71 The object of section 144 appears both from its own terms and from the Government's stated reasons for seeking its enactment by Parliament, as set out in the Response to Consultation. Although that response was not in formal terms a White Paper, in substance it fulfilled the same role of explaining the background to a legislative proposal introduced by the Government. In my view, therefore, the consultation paper has similar status to a White Paper as a legitimate aid to interpretation of section 144, and in particular as a legitimate source for guidance as to the policy objective which was sought to be achieved by section 144 (cf *Black Clawson International Ltd v Papierwerke Waldhof-Aschaffenburg AG* [1975] AC 591). The stated objective of section 144 was to provide deterrence and practical, on the ground assistance for home-owners in removing squatters from their property. Disruption of the law of adverse possession was not mentioned as an intended effect of the provision, nor was it suggested that it was being introduced to try to re-balance the rights of property owners as against those of adverse possessors with respect to the entitlement to be treated as title-holder in relation to property.
>
> 72 Although the Response to Consultation set out, in the summaries of various responses, the point made by the Land Registry regarding possible effects on the law of adverse possession, that was not something which the Government said anything about in its own explanation why it proposed to introduce the legislation.
>
> 73 The terms of section 144 make no reference to the adverse possession regimes for either registered land or unregistered land. Had there been any policy intention to affect either of those regimes by passing section 144, this would have been a very surprising omission. Acceptance of the Registrar's arguments would have a profoundly disruptive effect in relation to what has been the long established effect of the law of adverse possession for the purposes of acquiring title for both registered and unregistered land. It is not plausible to suppose that Parliament would have been silent about the impact of a provision like section 144 on the delicate and comprehensive balance of interests set out in the Limitation Act 1980 and in Schedule 6 to the LRA, had it truly intended that section 144 should have any impact at all on those regimes.
>
> 74 Although one could identify potentially significant differences in the relevant balance of public policy factors as between

1 At [64].

unregistered land and registered land – since the operation of the law of limitation and adverse possession is even more important in relation to unregistered land as the basis to show current title for the purposes of selling land – both counsel, for their own separate reasons, argued that the Registrar's argument would have a similar impact upon both registered and unregistered land. This would be very disruptive. The Registrar's argument, if correct, would mean that for registered land no-one could be sure that the title entered on the Register as a result of adverse possession was in fact a true title; someone (e.g. the former owner) might come forward at any later date and raise a case that part of the period of adverse possession was in fact affected by violation of section 144, so that the register ought to be rectified by reason of a mistake of the Registrar in accepting the application for registration of that title. The effect of the argument would also include disruption to the operation of the defence of adverse possession to a claim for possession of land as set out in section 98 of the LRA, opening up what on the face of it is a relatively simple factual inquiry whether a requisite period of adverse possession has been established, into an investigation into the quality of the adverse possession and whether the acts included any violations of section 144. The effect of the argument would be even more disruptive in relation to title to unregistered land, where title based on adverse possession critically depends upon the operation of sections 15 and 17 of the Limitation Act 1980. Section 17, in particular, was intended to provide assurance of good title in any case where the chain of title might conceivably include a relevant period of adverse possession: see Megarry and Wade, The Law of Real Property, 8th ed. (2012) by C. Harpum, S. Bridge and M. Dixon, para. 35-001. But that assurance would be undermined if what appeared to be a period of valid adverse possession could be attacked on the basis of allegations of breach of section 144 on facts potentially going back many years.

75 In the circumstances, I consider that the true inference is that in enacting section 144 Parliament did not intend to produce any collateral effect upon the settled law of adverse possession in respect of either registered or unregistered land.'

7–130K *Best* has therefore largely clarified the law in line with the position suggested in the Main Work at 7–139. Although Sales LJ was clear that he was adopting a 'narrower', and not the wide, approach to illegality, and although his judgment is an assessment of s 144 (and not any other criminal offence) against the policies behind adverse possession, it would appear from his reliance on the cases at paragraph [64] of his judgment, and the width of the policy grounds supporting adverse possession, that it will be difficult in future to argue that the illegality in the acts of possession relied upon by the squatter himself are to be excluded on the basis of the *ex turpi causa* defence. The examples which are cited of possibly relevant illegality disentitling a squatter from relying on illegal conduct – such as murdering the true owner (at paragraph [67]) are all examples of illegal conduct intended to conceal or avoid the consequences of the offences committed, and are not acts of possession in themselves. However it is also to be expected that a more open-textured, policy-based approach to illegality is likely to make it difficult to advise on the precise effect of criminal conduct. However, as a general statement of principle, it would seem that in most cases, the mere fact that an act of possession is illegal will not preclude a squatter from relying on it in an application to be registered.

7–130L That general statement requires immediate qualification, however the potential for difficulty in determining when criminal conduct is relevant, and when it is not, is clear from *Best* itself and the treatment of *R (Smith) v The Land Registry* [2009] EWHC 328 (Admin). What *Best* said about *Smith* was (1) that nothing in that latter case could be used to divine the intention of Parliament in relation to s 144 and that *Smith* did not set up some general rule of law, and (2) that *Smith* concerned a different statutory provision – s 137 of the Highways Act 1980, which restricted how a particular kind of land – highway – was to be used generally:

> '[91] In light of this discussion of *Bakewell Management*, I turn to consider Mr Karas's submission based on the first instance decision in *R (Smith) v The Land Registry*. In my view, it is not an authority which advances the case of the Registrar, for two reasons. First, a first instance decision the reasoning in which was not endorsed by the Court of Appeal, which chose to determine the case by reference to a different analysis, is too fragile a foundation on which to base any argument that Parliament, when enacting section 144 of LASPOA, must be taken somehow positively to have endorsed the alternative reasoning of HHJ Pelling QC. The first instance decision in that case tells us nothing about what Parliament intended should be the effect of section 144 in relation to the LRA.
>
> [92] Secondly, the reasoning of HHJ Pelling QC is not in fact inconsistent with the narrower submission advanced by Mr Rainey. The Judge followed the analysis in Bakewell Management, but found that he was dealing with a general provision of the criminal law which would have prevented the land-owner himself from using the land in the way the alleged adverse possessor had used it: see para. [14] of the judgment, referring to Lord Scott's opinion in *Bakewell Management* and *Glamorgan County Council v Carter*. As explained above, that is not the position in relation to section 144 of LASPOA.'

7–130M It will therefore remain the case that the policy of each individual Act will need to be looked at. It may be that enactments which do not merely render a particular form of conduct by a particular class of individuals illegal, but which have the policy of preserving land in a particular state (for instance, unenclosed) for some public purpose, will continue to form the basis of an illegality defence.[1]

1 For a recent decision where village greens and illegality were tangentially considered, see *Wapham v London Borough of Hillingdon* REF/2016/0085.

7–136A In *Couper v Albion Properties Limited* [2013] EWHC 2993 (Ch), at [611]–[614], it was held that adverse possession of the bed of a river subject to a right of public navigation, with the riverbed vested in the Port of London Authority by statute, was impossible, following the reasoning in *R (Smith) v Land Registry* [2010] EWCA Civ 200.

7–136B By way of contrast, Judge Elizabeth Cooke decided that the right of public navigation would have made no difference to the claim in *Port of London Authority v Mendoza* [2017] UKUT 146 (TCC), though it failed for other reasons (see below, paragraphs 9–05A and 9–05B). She reviewed the navigation cases and stated (at paragraphs 78 and 81) that:

> 'I take the view that there can be no absolute rule that adverse possession is impossible on the bed of a river that is subject to public rights of navigation. Equally, those rights cannot be extinguished by adverse possession. In this case the Wight Queen [the boat in question] is moored on an arm of a river that is little used; public navigation happens in the wider channel on the other side of the long island in the midst of the river. Realistically the Wight Queen's presence has no effect upon the public in its exercise of its right to navigate. It is not necessary to adapt the law of adverse possession to cater for the case where a member of the public perversely insisted on taking a boat or a canoe, not along the open water, but across the very place where this boat is moored. That does not happen and there is no need for the law to bend to allow it to happen. At the other extreme it is not clear to me how it would be possible to take adverse possession of the whole width of a publicly navigable river, because the public rights of nav-igation would prevent factual possession.
>
> [...]
>
> In this case, therefore, had Mr Mendoza been able to establish not only factual possession but also intention to possess I would not have found that the public's right of navigation – undisturbed in fact by the Wight Queen's presence – would have made any difference to that. The analogy with the public highway breaks down because highways – which have to be completely open to traffic and pedestrians – are so very different from rivers. A closer analogy is perhaps to the adverse possession of land through which a public footpath runs (as in *JA Pye (Oxford) Ltd v Graham* [2003] 1 AC 419); adverse possession does not extinguish the footpath and the public's rights continue unabated on the path. Here the public's rights would have continued unabated over a wide stretch of river, unaffected by what amounts in effect to a very slight narrowing of the river so far as public navigation is concerned.'

7–141 In *Walton v Hedleyhope Parish Council* REF/2011/0399/0400 the Deputy Adjudicator, Mr Michell, rejected the claim on the facts. He said that if, contrary to his decision, the applicant had taken possession of the disputed land, which formed part of a village green, by fencing it and siting a caravan on it, he could not have relied on those acts as they were criminal offences under s 12 of the Inclosure Act 1857 and s 29 of the Commons Act 1876. The basis of the reasoning, which appears to accord with the later Supreme Court authorities referred to above, is that the public policy of ensuring village greens remain accessible is infringed by its (criminal) enclosure. Mr Michell said: '*The purpose of the sections in creating the criminal offences would appear to me to be to protect the practical ability of the public to enjoy the green without interruption. It is a criminal offence to do any act which injures the green or interrupts the use and enjoyment of the green for exercise and recreation and enclosing the green or part of it will interrupt that use and enjoyment while the fence is in place. The objective of enabling the public to enjoy the village green without interruption is better achieved, in my judgment, if squatters are not permitted to acquire title by relying on illegal fencing or other acts which are made illegal by the sections referred to. If squatters were to be permitted to rely on fencing a village green, there would be an incentive for them to do so and an increase in the risk of the public's rights to enjoy the green being interrupted. In the absence of authority to the contrary, I would therefore hold that Mr Walton cannot rely on illegal acts in seeking to show title by adverse possession to part of the village green*'. However, it is questionable to what extent this approach is justified and whether it sits happily with the outcome in *Best*.

On Charity Commission schemes, see *Martham Parish Council v Martham Boat Building and Development Company Limited* REF/2012/0595. On highways not maintainable at public expense, see *Bell v MacFarlane* REF/2013/0242. In relation to burial sites, see *Beavis v Bond* REF/2015/0043.

Chapter 8
The factual element of possession

8–13 In *Akhtar v Brewster* [2012] EWHC 3521 (Ch), at [97], it was held that the fact that there was a hiatus between acts of possession – in that case, gaps between mooring tenants – did not preclude a claim that the squatter was in possession.[1]

8–15A In *Chambers v London Borough of Havering* [2011] EWCA Civ 1576, at [25], Lewison LJ referred to the trial judge's holding that factual use by the squatter had been 'intermittent and not continuous', and that there was 'no continuous adverse use being made of the disputed land until about 2002' as 'not the legal test'. See too *Akhtar v Brewster & Anor*, above, paragraph 8–13; and *Boot v Bromford Housing Association Limited* [2017] UKFTT 0182 (PC) (Judge John Hewitt).

8–16 Add footnote at end of paragraph: This and the following paragraph from the First Edition of the Main Work were cited with approval in *Mellstrom v Badgworthy Land Company Limited* REF/2008/1498, 2009/0290, 2009/0953.

8–34 This approach was also adopted in *Norbrook Laboratories v Maguire* [2012] NICh 32, at [45].

1 The same point was considered in *Ngan Cheung Wah v Kwong Shook Ling* [2014] HKCA 567.

Chapter 9

The mental element of possession – the intention to possess

9–05A In *Port of London Authority v Mendoza* [2017] UKUT 146 (TCC), Judge Elizabeth Cooke was dealing with an adverse possession claim based on mooring to a pre-existing structure by a single boat. She reviewed the principles on equivocal conduct and approached the issue by asking whether the conduct of the putative squatter could be referable to some other right he might enjoy, such as a licence or as an ancillary right to the right of public navigation. She stated (at paragraphs [57] and [69]):

> 'The presence of a moored boat is as equivocal an act of possession as can be imagined. The casual observer, and likewise the paper owner, can know nothing of the boat owner's intention from the boat's presence. It is not possible to tell how long it has been there, how long the owner intends to stay, whether it is moored in exercise of an easement or of a public right, whether it is acquiring an easement, whether it has a licence to moor, or whether it is just trespassing, for a few days or a few months.
>
> The presence of a moored boat is as equivocal an act of possession as can be imagined. The casual observer, and likewise the paper owner, can know nothing of the boat owner's intention from the boat's presence. It is not possible to tell how long it has been there, how long the owner intends to stay, whether it is moored in exercise of an easement or of a public right, whether it is acquiring an easement, whether it has a licence to moor, or whether it is just trespassing, for a few days or a few months.
>
> It may be that it is in general very difficult for someone who intends to take adverse possession of the river bed by mooring a boat there to make that intention clear to the world. Mr Stonor QC suggested ways in which it might be done for example by putting up a sign saying "private land and mooring" or by putting a construction on the river bed to support the boat when moored. I make no comment on the ways in which it might be done; but it has to be done and it was not done here.'

9–05B It appears that the principal reason for rejecting Mr Mendoza's claim was therefore that the acts were too slight. In particular, it would seem that the mere act of mooring is, without more, not capable of amounting to exclusive possession, though in other cases the putative squatter may also be able to point to other acts on top of mooring, such as enclosing and building on a section of the adjacent bank, to strengthen the claim. It would, it is respectfully suggested, be wrong to seek to extract from *Mendoza* a wider principle that if exclusive possession is found which is adverse, such possession may still be equivocal if it could be explained by reference to some private right that might have been (but was not) granted by a third party, or some public right. Insofar as it remains a useful test, comparing the conduct of the squatter with what acts would have been authorised by some lesser right sheds light on whether the acts amount to possession and filters out marginal cases. The test should have no application, however, where the tribunal is satisfied on the facts that there is exclusive possession.

9–28 Add to Fn 32: *Curatus Trust Company (Mauritius) Limited v London Borough of Wandsworth* REF/2011/0260.

9–42 *Hughes v Cork* has been followed repeatedly in Hong Kong: see *Cheung KwongYuen v Sun Hui Fang* [2015] HKCA 564, and the first instance cases there cited.

9–51 In *Gill v McCarthy* REF/2014/0495; 0661; 0838, Judge Hewitt considered that this issue was settled by *Alston* at any level below the Court of Appeal. Regrettably the cases were not considered by the Privy Council in *Smith v Molyneaux* [2016] UKPC 35.

9–89A The High Court has found twice that the use of land for mooring boats did not sufficiently demonstrate the *animus possidendi* as such use could be consistent with the exercise of an easement to do the same: see *Couper v Albion Properties Ltd* [2013] EWHC 2993 at [507] and [522] and *Port of London v Tower Bridge Yacht and Boat Company Limited* [2013] EWHC 3084 (Ch), at [281]–[285]. For a detailed discussion of this issue see *Port of London Authority v Mendoza* [2017] UKUT 146 (TCC), and see the quoted text above, paragraphs 9–05A and 9–05B of this Update.

9–126A In *Armbrister v Lightbourn* [2012] UKPC 40, at [83], the Privy Council considered it relevant that the squatter mistakenly believed he was the true owner, and had acted on that belief.

9–126B In *Couper v Albion Properties Ltd* [2013] EWHC 2993, the putative squatter's claim for possession of a river wall section failed, firstly on the factual element of possession, but also because he had repeatedly professed the view (and hence manifested a subjective intention) that the wall, which was used for mooring, was used on a common and non-exclusive basis with the true owner, and that this was the manner in which the squatter used and intended to use it: see at [520]–[523].

9–126C In *Tsoukkas v Southwark Council* REF 2012/0049, a squatter believed that he had a right of way. In fact, the squatter behaved more expansively than that. The Deputy Adjudicator, Mr Ryhs, said: '… *a belief that the Applicant had a right of way over the land is not inconsistent with an intention to possess the land, given that his use of the Yard was clearly outside the scope of any easement. Enjoyment of a right of way does not, by definition, amount to exclusive factual possession, but the intention to possess the Yard may be inferred from the actual use made of it by the Applicant, coupled with the physical exclusion of everyone else*'.

9–127 Add footnote to paragraph 1: see *Port of London Authority v Mendoza* [2017] UKUT 146 (TCC) at paragraph [69].

Add footnote to paragraph 2: *Port of London Authority v Mendoza* [2017] UKUT 146 (TCC) at paragraph [83].

9–154A That the *Leigh v Jack* approach remains heretical was re-confirmed by the Court of Appeal in *Chambers v London Borough of Havering* [2011] EWCA Civ 1576, [35]–[36].

Chapter 10

The extent of possession: when possession of part of the surface will be treated as possession of whole

10–08A It has been held that title by adverse possession can be obtained in respect of part of the bed of a river. In *Port of London v Tower Bridge Yacht and Boat Company Limited* [2013] EWHC 3084, Mann J stated as follows at paragraph 278:

(a) It seems that possession can be taken of the river bed by activities amounting to mooring. In *PLA v Ashmore* (supra) the claim was to the area of river bed on which a boat rested at low tide. On some assumed facts it was held that adverse possession of the bed could be acquired of the area represented by the footprint of the boat. It is true that the actual decision to that effect in the case was overturned by the Court of Appeal as being one which was procedurally unsound, but Mr Harpum did not really challenge the principle on which the first instance decision proceeded. In *Moore v BWB* Lewison LJ seemed to accept that one could acquire title by adverse possession of a part of the river bed by mooring a vessel in the waters above it – see para 57.

(b) It is possible adversely to possess, and then acquire a possessory title of, a space which does not include the land below or the airspace above. Thus in that way one can acquire a possessory title of a tunnel (*Bevan v London Portland Cement Co Ltd* (1892) 67 LT 615 or horizontal part of a building such as a flat (*Ramroop v Ishmael* [2010] UKPC 14). There is therefore nothing inherently legally impossible in a claim for adverse possession for a very limited part of the subsoil.

(c) Possessory title can be obtained of a very small piece of land. This not infrequently happens where there is a minor encroachment by a small part of foundations.

Add footnote to end of sub-paragraph (a): In *Port of London Authority v Mendoza* [2017] UKUT 146 (TCC) it was considered that mooring was unlikely ever to amount to adverse possession, however, as merely mooring was equivocal as to the *animus possidendi*. However, it was acknowledged that each case might turn on its facts and a claim based on mooring might succeed if supported by other acts for possession.

Add footnote to end of sub-paragraph (b): see also *Abbott v Thomas* REF/2009/1139.

10–08B It has been held in Hong Kong that it is not possible to acquire title to the external surface of a wall, either by grant or by adverse possession. In *Sunbroad Holdings v All Occupiers (Whose Names Are Unknown)* [2012] HKCA 133, a cobbler attached some boxes and a canopy to the external surface of a wall which did not belong to him and then used them for a very long time. His claim to adverse possession failed. It had previously been held by the Hong Kong Courts that it is not possible to have a lease of the surface of the outer wall of a building because it has no horizontal dimension: see *Leung Kwok Kau v Tam So Wa* [1968] HKLR 673: '*In the absence of a defined portion of the soil, to which a letting can be distinctly related, no lease or tenancy can arise. Where the subject matter of an alleged lease or tenancy is but the bare surface of such a wall, it has no width or breadth of soil to support it, as a lease or tenancy. No estate or interest in land is created; I use the word 'land' in its widest sense,*' per Mills-Owens J at 679. For the same reason, in *Sunbroad*, the Hong Kong Court of Appeal held that there could be no adverse possession of the surface of a wall. There is no English authority on the issue, and it is questionable whether the same approach would be taken. Many so-called 'eggshell' leases of flats and offices define the demised premises as including only the internal decorative finishes of the demised space: see eg *Pumperninks of Piccadilly Ltd v Land Securities Plc* [2002] Ch 332. Provided a vertical surface is capable of being the subject of exclusive use and control, it seems well arguable that title to it can be granted or acquired by adverse possession.

10–29 The *unum quid* principle was discussed in *Franklin v Smith* REF/2013/0265/0264 and *Mills v Rapley* REF/2014/0317, and in particular the common locality test is discussed at [30]. The principle was applied to the acquisition of prescriptive rights in *Lynn Shellfish Ltd v Loose* [2016] UKSC 14, where Lord Neuberger and Lord Carnwath for the majority, having expressed the general position that the extent of a prescriptive right is dictated by the use which generated it, stated as follows:

> '46. […] the extent of the right obtained by prescription has to be established bearing in mind practical reality. This is exemplified by the unum quid rule which was explained by Lord Blackburn (who said that it was "as much the law in a Scotch as in an English Court") in Lord Advocate and the Trustees of the Clyde Navigation v Lord Blantyre (1879) 4 App Cas 770, 791-792 in these terms: "[A]ll that tends to prove possession as owners of parts of the tract tends to prove ownership of the whole tract; provided that there is such common character of locality as would raise a reasonable inference that if the barons possessed one part as owners they possessed the whole, the weight depending on the nature of the tract, what kind of possession could be had of it, and what kind of possession was proved."
>
> 47. This was said in connection with possession and ownership of land, but it applies equally to rights over land…'.

Chapter 11

The extent of possession: mines and minerals

11–02 The law on title to mines and minerals is discussed in the Law Commission CP 227 at 3.18ff.

Chapter 12

Possession of specific types of land

12–08 The fencing cases are discussed further in *Heaney v Kirkby* [2015] UKUT 0178 (TCC), at [30].

12–17A In *Armbrister v Lightbourn* [2012] UKPC 40, at [83], the Privy Council advised that the fact that the land in question was remote and unsuitable for cultivation was a factor influencing them in favour of the squatter, whose acts of possession had been limited to some sharecropping.

12–27 Add (11) Mooring a vessel; '... *it seems to be possible to acquire title by adverse possession of a river bed by mooring a vessel in the waters above it: The Port of London Authority v Ashmore [2010] EWCA Civ 30 [2010] 1 All ER 1139*', per Lewison LJ in *Moore v British Waterways Board* [2013] EWCA Civ 73 at [57]. The *Ashmore* case is discussed in the Main Work at 12–31 to 12–33; see also *Port of London v Tower Bridge Yacht and Boat Company Limited* [2013] EWHC 3084, at [268] and [278(a)] (where the proposition was not disputed). The fullest recent decision is *Port of London Authority v Mendoza* [2017] UKUT 146 (TCC).

12–33A In *Couper v Albion Properties Ltd* [2013] EWHC 2993 the Port of London Authority accepted for the purposes of the trial (reserving its position on any appeal, see at [600]) that *Ashmore* was correct in holding that it is possible to obtain adverse possession of the riverbed by means of a vessel which sits on the riverbed at low tide and rises with the tide. Arnold J held that the fact that a particular anchor was not continuously in use was not fatal to the claim, but a claim could only succeed in respect of anchors in the same location. However the claim failed as Arnold J held that it is not possible as a matter of law to establish adverse possession of that part of the bed of the Thames which is vested in the Port of London Authority by statute for the purposes of, among other things, regulating the public right of navigation of the river; the position was therefore the same as with a highway vested in a highways authority, as to which see the Main Work at 7–136: see at [611] to [613]. This was not a point argued in *Ashmore*.

12–33B In *Port of London v Tower Bridge Yacht and Boat Company Limited* [2013] EWHC 3084, the claim was not to the space occupied by moored vessels, but only to the space in the bed of the river occupied by mooring roots (ie the blocks or anchors embedded in the riverbed to which vessels are tied up when moored). On the facts of that case, Mann J pointed out that the fact that the space claimed was small did not itself rule out the claim but did mean it should be carefully considered: [270].

He acknowledged that it is possible adversely to possess, and then acquire a possessory title of, a space which does not include the land below or the airspace above, eg a tunnel and that possessory title can be obtained of a very small piece of land, eg a minor encroachment by a small part of foundations: [278]. However, he rejected the adverse possession claim in that case for two reasons:

(1) the acts relied on did not amount to factual possession, which requires some sort of physical presence or at least being in physical control in some real way; an anchor or block placed in the riverbed is put there to facilitate the activity of mooring above (at [280]–[283]).
(2) there had been no identification of the precise location of the land claimed: '*Someone claiming a possessory title (as I shall call it, for the sake of convenience) should be able to point to the physical extent of the land to which possession is claimed… if you cannot point out what land you are claiming adverse possession of, you cannot get a declaration that you are entitled to anything in particular*': see at [273]–[274].

12–33C In *Port of London Authority v Mendoza* [2017] UKUT 146 (TCC), in the context of a case in which a single boat was moored to an existing structure, Judge Elizabeth Cooke reviewed all the authorities on adverse possession and mooring, and decided as follows:

(1) *Ashmore* (see Main Work at 12–31) could not be treated as having decided definitively whether the mooring of a boat amounted to adverse possession. Nor had the point been decided in *Denaby and Cadeby Main Collieries Ltd v Anson* [1911] 1 KB 171, *Fowler v Gafford* [1968] 2 QB 618 and *Roberts v Swangrove Estates Ltd* [2007] 2 P & CR 17. Those cases were in any event distinguishable from the facts in *Mendoza*.
(2) That the act of mooring was likely to be equivocal in most cases and hence would not found a claim in adverse possession in most cases: see above, 9–05A and 9–05B.

12–39A Use of a river wall for mooring with others does not amount to possession of the wall: *Couper v Albion Properties Ltd* [2013] EWHC 2993. Care must also be taken to ascertain whether the wall is a party structure or not: *Rashid v Sharif* [2014] EWCA Civ 377. In *Sunbroad Holdings v All Occupiers (Whose Names Are Unknown)* [2012] HKCA 133 it was held that it is not possible to acquire title to the external surface of a wall – see 10–08B above.

12–39B For consideration of difficulties with adverse possession of hedges, see *Avon Estates Limited v Evans* [2013] EWHC 1635 (Ch).

12–41 Add to Fn 84: Deputy Adjudicator Owen Rhys came to the same conclusion under the Commons Registration Act 1965, in *Mellstrom v Badgworthy Land Company Limited* REF/2008/1498, 2009/0290, 2009/0953, though that was a case in which there was no enclosure and the claim to adverse possession failed on its facts. See in particular the analysis at [35] and [45]–[49].

Chapter 13

Whether specific uses of land constitute possession

13–01 Fn 1: the 'holistic' approach is well-illustrated by *Akhtar v Brewster* [2012] EWHC 3521 (Ch).

13–03 This paragraph, and those following to 13.08, were approved in *Akhtar v Brewster* [2012] EWHC 3521 (Ch), at [100]. They are further discussed by Newey J in *Harrison & Anor v Brading* [2016] EWHC 3267 (Ch).

13–14A The erection of a fence was decisive in the case of *McGuinness v Preece* [2016] EWHC 1518 (Ch), at [56]–[58]. The lack of a fence was decisive in *Mellstrom v Badgworthy Land Company Limited* REF/2008/1498, 2009/0290, 2009/0953, a case concerning commons, which was contrasted with *Whitehurst v Dickinson* REF/2008/0315, also a commons case, but on that occasion successful due to the fact of enclosure by fence.

13–17A In *Chambers v London Borough of Havering* [2011] EWCA Civ 1576, the Court of Appeal held that the trial judge's assessment of evidence about whether an occupier's use of land for grazing animals, including the placing of moveable shelters and the repair and replacement of fencing, amounted to adverse possession was flawed. Etherton LJ (at [37]–[40]) discussed *Minchinton* and *Inglewood* and said he thought there was no inconsistency between them on the significance of fencing and that they did not show a different approach in principle. Lewison LJ also discussed the cases (at [63]–[69]) said he thought that the approach in *Minchinton* had been right. Rix LJ (at [73]) found it unnecessary to resolve the differences between Etherton and Lewison LJJ in order to dispose of the appeal. The *Minchinton* approach was applied in *Harber v London Borough of Havering* REF/2014/0543; and see *Leinum v Crawford* REF/2014/0790.

13–17B A different problem arose in *Rashid v Sharif* [2014] EWCA Civ 377. In that case, R and S lived in abutting properties. The original wooden fence separating them had been taken down by R's predecessors in title and replaced by a brick wall. S had demolished the wall to erect a shed, with the rear wall of the shed on the footprint of the old wall. R claimed for trespass on the basis that, *inter alia*, the wall was his by adverse possession, having been erected and maintained by his predecessor. However, the evidence was that the wall was erected not on R's land alone, but as a party fence wall straddling the boundary. Insofar as the wall was on S's land, and subject to the Party Wall etc Act 1996, there was no trespass. A boundary structure enclosing land may not, therefore, belong to the person who built it and may not amount to adverse possession of its footprint in that person's favour.

13–18 For a further illustration of the difficulties of adversely possessing a hedge, see *Avon Estates Limited v Evans* [2013] EWHC 1635 (Ch).

13–22A As to the erection of a pillar as part of a boundary wall and gate, see *Bradley v Heslin* [2014] EWHC 3267 (Ch). The fencing cases (and the implications of a lack of fencing) are discussed further in *Heaney v Kirkby* [2015] UKUT 0178 (TCC), at [30].

13–29 It is not a requirement of 'for time to run' that there is complete enclosure so that the land becomes inaccessible to all apart from the squatter: see *Greenmanor v Pilford* [2012] EWCA Civ 756 at [27]. For a further case on the significance of walls and fences, see *Norbrook Laboratories v Maguire* [2012] NICh 32.

13–38 A further illustration of a 'waste strip' adverse possession case is *Heaney v Kirkby* [2015] UKUT 0178 (TCC), where it seems possible that less exacting evidence of possession is required in practice.

13–40 Add to Fn 78: see *Dyer v Dyer* [2013] EWHC 209 (Ch), discussing these authorities, and affirming that (a) each case turns on its own facts and (b) that there may be differences in the manner in which land is cared for which might be decisive, and which, on the facts of that case, resulted in the squatter succeeding in relation to some parcels of land but not others.

13–49 This paragraph is cited with approval in *Tsoi Ping Hung v Cheung Chow Lan* [2015] HKCA 197, applying the cases cited.

13–57 See too *Rashid v Sharif* [2014] EWCA Civ 377.

13–60 This paragraph and the next were cited with approval in *Gotland Enterprises Limited v Kwok Chi Yau* [2016] HKCA 25. See too *Lee Theatre Realty Ltd v Tong WahJor* [2013] HKCA 215.

13–63 This judgment was upheld on appeal in relation to other points in *Baxter v Mannion* [2011] EWCA Civ 120.

13–67A The character of the land meant that grazing carried some weight in *Chambers v London Borough of Havering* [2011] EWCA Civ 1576, at [54] and [56], though a retrial was ordered to determine the issue finally. Grazing was not sufficient in *Avon Estates Limited v Evans* [2013] EWHC 1635 (Ch).

13–70 See also *Balevents Ltd v Sartori* [2014] EWHC 1164 (Ch), at [89]–[94].

13–73 See also *Hopkins v Haynes* REF/2013/0499/0501.

13–77 Add to Fn 178: compare the discussion at first instance in *Parshall v Bryans* [2012] EWHC 665 (Ch).

13–80A Parking was found to be insufficient in *Nata Lee Ltd v Abid* [2014] EWCA Civ 1652. Briggs LJ stated as follows:

> '37. The judge relied upon parking on the disputed land, upon the assumption by the owners of No. 105 of responsibility for its maintenance, and (perhaps) upon the painting of the black line. Her conclusion, at paragraph 29, that "the claimants and their predecessors in title clearly intended to and did possess the land in question and in doing so excluded the legal owners…" appears to accord with the legal requirement for exclusion of the paper title owner, but I have been unable to understand how parking, maintenance and the painting of the black line did so in fact.
>
> 38. Taking each element in turn, it is evident from the photographs that parking on the disputed land did not occupy the whole of it, still less exclude the owners of No. 99 from using it as a means of access to the side of their warehouse. The photographs show that, prior to the demolition of the warehouse, there was some form of aperture in it further down the yard, probably beyond the disputed land, to which the owners of No. 99 would have needed to use the disputed land for gaining access. The assumption of a responsibility for maintenance appears, on the evidence to which I have referred, to have been very limited. Maintenance appears to have amounted to little more than keeping the disputed land clean and tidy. Finally, the painting of the black line was not carried out by the owners of No. 105 at all, but by Mr. Garfield while he was the owner of No. 99. Taking his evidence as a whole, it appears that he did it so as to mark out the furthest limit of the permitted parking by the owners of No. 105, in such a way as to ensure that it did not interfere with his access to what he called his "shutter" which appears to have been a large opening into the warehouse (different from the one which I have just described) which had been bricked up before the relevant photographs were taken. Far from being an act of possession or exclusion by the claimant sufficient for adverse possession, painting the black line was something done for a quite different purpose by the paper title owner, and did not in any way exclude his continuing access to the disputed land.
>
> 39. Taking the three elements of conduct relied upon in the aggregate points no more to the exclusion of the owners of No. 99 from the disputed land than does a review of each of them separately. For those reasons, I consider that the judge was wrong to find that the owners of No. 105 acquired adverse possession of the disputed land.'

Mooring Boats

13–80B There has been a great deal of litigation about the mooring of boats, and the adverse possession consequences of that: see the cases discussed in Chapter 12 of the Main Work and this Update. It seems from the cases cited above that there are a number of ways in which an adverse possession claim might be advanced on the basis of mooring and associated conduct:

(1) That the mooring of a boat amounts to possession of the column of water and riverbed beneath it, particularly when the waters are tidal and the boat settles on the bed at low tide. This may be susceptible to counter arguments based on the right of public navigation and the vesting of the bed of the river in a public authority by statute.
(2) That the mooring of a boat amounts to possession of the space occupied by the anchor and the boat to which it is attached.
(3) That the mooring of the boat amounts to adverse possession of the entire part of the bank or shore co-extensive with mooring activity, although this would appear to require additional conduct on shore, such as control of the riverbank.
(4) That the mooring of boats amounts to adverse possession of the space occupied by the mooring equipment on the bank or shore. This is susceptible to the counter argument that the use is mere use falling short of possession, even if the land claimed is small.

13–80C It appears in principle possible to establish that the mooring of a boat on the water can amount to adverse possession of the river bed under it, at any rate if the water is tidal, though the point has largely been assumed to be correct at first instance, and the proposition remains to be properly tested by the Court of Appeal: see the cases at paragraphs 12–29 and following of the Main Work and this Update. However, adverse possession of the outline of the anchor and chain, or of the mooring ropes and fixtures, seems more difficult to establish, being regarded by the courts as use rather than possession. It is only if conduct goes further than this that the adverse possession may succeed.[1] Illegality issues in relation to waters subject to the public rights of navigation are considered in Chapter 7.

1 *Akhtar v Brewster* [2012] EWHC 3521 (Ch).

Chapter 14

How long must time run for?

14–06 The question of what constitutes the 'Crown' for these purposes was considered in *Scott v Arrandene Limited* REF/2013/0712, holding that the Official Receiver was not the Crown.

Chapter 15
What will stop time running?

15–03 Add to Fn 3: as to the effect of proceedings about title before the Adjudicator, see *Secretary of State for Transport v Quest Maidstone* REF/2010/0210 at [27].

Add to Fn 4: For an example of interruption by demolition of a squatter's structure, see *Abbott v Thomas* REF/2009/1139.

15–03A In *Zarb v Parry* [2011] EWCA Civ 1306, the paper title owner had undertaken acts, such as erecting posts and laying a surveyor's tape, which had the incontrovertible intention behind them of re-taking possession, but physical possession was not re-taken as the paper title owner was met with objections from the squatter and relented. Were those acts nonetheless sufficient of an interruption of the squatter's exclusive possession? The Court of Appeal considered *Bligh v Martyn* [1968] 1 WLR 804 (see paragraph 7–67 of the Main Work) and then stated as follows (at [43]):

> 'The facts in *Bligh v Martin* were very different from those of the present case. This appeal is concerned with part of a garden, not farmland. Pennycuick J did not have to consider the effect of an attempt to retake possession that had been thwarted by the adverse possessor, or abandoned. Nor did he have to consider the effect of an oral declaration of intent by the paper title owner communicated to the adverse possessor. In my judgment, however, the principle on which *Bligh* was decided, namely that the factual possession of the adverse possessor must be brought to an end is clearly correct and determines the result on this issue. The principle achieves a simple test for ascertaining whether the period of adverse possession has been brought to an end. Interruption will be overt and so it can be more easily proved or disproved if the question has to be litigated many years later. Furthermore, if the paper title owner did something less than exclude the adverse possessor, such as plant a flag, put up a notice or make an oral declaration of ownership, the adverse possessor would continue to have factual possession in the sense defined in *Pye*. A person might, therefore, continue to have the intent to possess and factual possession throughout the period of any interruption of his adverse possession by symbolic acts such as I have mentioned. It would, in my judgment, be inconsistent with *Pye* if an adverse possessor could at one and the same time fulfil the requirements for adverse possession but yet have his possession effectively interrupted by the paper title owner. Finally, there is no need for the paper title owner to know that he is bringing the adverse possession to an end or to say that he is doing so: it is the quality of the acts which matters and not any oral declarations.'

15–04 In the absence of a personal representative, the emergency measures set out in *Best v Curtis* REF/2015/0130 may need to be taken.

Who Has A Right to Recover Land By Possession Proceedings?

15–04A Evidently, a person with a legal estate – be it a fee simple or a term of years – has a right to possession. However, possession claims are no longer restricted to those two classes of person. The Court of Appeal has held that a licensee might have a sufficient amount of control of a site to be said to be in possession of it: see *Manchester Airport v Dutton* [2000] 1 QB 133.[1] It has further been decided *obiter* at Adjudicator level that the imposition of a statutory scheme over land, vesting possession by operation of statute in one entity whilst leaving ownership vested in the original owner, has the effect of making the owner's interest take effect as an estate in reversion: see *Whitehurst v Dickinson* [2009] EWLandRA 2008_0315 (27 July 2009),[2] so that the position is the same as that which applies to a squatter taking adverse possession of land subject to a lease.

15–04B Although not concerned with adverse possession, the point in relation to possession claims arose in *Hall v Mayor of London (On Behalf of the Greater London Authority)* [2010] EWCA Civ 817,[3] the Court of Appeal considered in detail the question of who has the right to possession. It rejected as 'arcane' the argument that only a person who would have been capable of maintaining an action for ejectment could bring a possession claim. Referring to *Secretary of State for Environment, Food, and Rural Affairs v Meier* [2009] UKSC 11 and *Manchester Airport v Dutton* [2000] 1 QB 133, Lord Neuberger MR explained at [27] that:

> '[...] there is obvious force in the point that the modern law relating to possession claims should not be shackled by the arcane and archaic rules relating to ejectment, and, in particular, that it should develop and adapt to accommodate a claim by anyone entitled to use and control, effectively amounting to possession, of the land in question – along the lines of the views expressed by Laws LJ in *Dutton* [2000] 1 QB 133 and by Lady Hale in *Meier* [2009] 1 WLR 2780. Further, it is only my opinion in *Meier* [2009] 1 WLR 2780, paragraphs 60-69, which can be said plainly to support the argument that a possession order may be subject to the same principles as those that applied to ejectment, and even my opinion was concerned with a very different aspect of a possession order from that raised here, as the claimant's title was not in issue. Lord Rodger at [2009] 1 WLR 2780, paragraphs 6 and 7, can be said to provide only a little, and then only very indirect, support for the argument, and any such support is rather undermined by his uncritical citation of *Dutton* [2000] 1 QB 133.

1 Compare, however, *Countryside Residential (North Thames) Ltd v Tugwell* [2000] 2 EGLR 59.
2 [75] and following; a decision of Deputy Adjudicator Stephen Jourdan QC.
3 The decision to make the possession order can be found in *The Mayor of London (Greater London Authority) v Haw* [2011] EWHC 585 (QB).

The effect of the brief speeches of Lord Walker and Lord Collins is neutral on the argument, save that they can be said to have adopted a relatively orthodox approach to the concept of possession. Lady Hale's observations at [2009] 1 WLR 2780, paragraphs 26-36 are rather against the argument.'

15–04C The issue in *Hall* was whether an action for possession could be brought by the Mayor – and not the Crown, in whom ownership of the land was vested – against the protesters located on Parliament Square Gardens. The Mayor had statutory duties to manage that land under the Greater London Authority Act 1999, s 384, and had a power to make byelaws to control, prohibit and permit use of the Gardens under s 385. These statutory rights, taken as a whole, amounted to possession when taken as a whole, even without the vesting in the Mayor of legal title to an estate in land, carrying with it the right to possession. Lord Neuberger explained this effect at [21]:

> 'The powers and duties relating to PSG and conferred on the Greater London Authority (which I shall treat as conferred on the Mayor, both in the light of section 384(8) and for the sake of convenience) are in sections 384(3) and (4), 385(1) and (2), and the Byelaws. In my view, those provisions, as can be seen from the control which the Mayor actually exercised (gardening, refuse collection, patrolling, enforcement of by-laws), inevitably lead to the conclusion that the Mayor was, at any rate until 1 May, in possession of PSG. As the majority of the Australian High Court put it, a person has possession of certain land if he can "control access to the [land] by others, and, in general, decide how the land will be used" – *Western Australia v Ward* (2002) 213 CLR 1, paragraph 52. Of course, the grassed area of PSG is not fenced off, as it is intended to be available for general public access, but the precise nature of the acts and rights required to amount to possession varies with the nature of the land and all the circumstances – see e.g. *West Bank Estates Ltd v Arthur* [1967] 1 AC 665, 678B–C.'

15–04D It may therefore be necessary, when dealing with land in relation to which a statutory management scheme exists, to consider:

(1) Whether the scheme renders the acts of the putative squatter illegal so that they cannot found a claim for adverse possession at all, as to which see paragraphs 7–130ff of the main work and paragraphs 7–130Aff of this Supplement for the law as it now stands.
(2) If not, whether the scheme operates so as to confer exclusive possession upon the entity charged with the management of the land, so that it can be determined whether time runs against the statutory right holder or the true legal owner.

15–04E If time is running against the underlying owner, then the squatter will, it is considered, be entitled to become registered with that title but subject to the terms of the statutory scheme which remains in force. If time is running against the statutory right holder, then it is considered that the issue is more difficult. The squatter may evidently not be registered with the statutory right to possession. Although this precise issue appears not to have been contemplated by the draftsman, we consider that s 15(1) is wide enough to allow a squatter to defend against a possession action brought on a statutory basis, as such a person is 'any person' and the action is plainly an 'action to recover land' within the meaning of the Limitation Act 1980, s 15(1).

15–04F If statute vests title to land in a public authority then the first question is whether the statutory vesting is inconsistent with the operation of the statutes governing adverse possession (as has been held to be the case with highways and the bed of the Thames vested in the Port of London Authority). If not, there is no reason why the Limitation Act 1980 and the Land Registration Act 2002 should not operate in the normal way. It is less clear what the position is if the statutory scheme does not vest ownership in an authority, but rather vests all the incidents of ownership including the right to control access and seek possession. It seems likely that in such a case the statutory provisions would be regarded as inconsistent with the operation of the statutes governing adverse possession.

15–19 See also the discussion in *Grand Wayfair Investment Company Limited v Chan Yung Kan* [2014] HKCA 481.

Chapter 16

Extension of time by acknowledgment or payment

16–44 In *Secretary of State for Transport v Quest Maidstone* REF/2010/0210, a conditional offer to buy was contained in a letter sent to the District Valuer, which was forwarded on to the true owner. The Deputy Adjudicator decided that this letter was an acknowledgment, and that the manner in which it had come to be passed to the true owner amounted to an acknowledgment 'to' him. He decided that, following *Rehman v Benfield* [2006] EWCA Civ 1392, and the earlier case of *Re Compania de Electricidad* [1980] Ch 146, that this indirect making of an acknowledgment was sufficient under the Limitation Act 1980. Acknowledgment to a person without title at the time of the acknowledgment will not do: *Faccey v Bedford Borough Council* REF/2014/0022. See further *Yu Kit Chiu v Chan Shek Woo* [2011] HKCA 27.

16–67 In *Curatus Trust Company (Mauritius) Limited v London Borough of Wandsworth* REF/2011/0260, it appears to be suggested at [22] that an offer to take a licence might not be an acknowledgment. However, it is considered that this would be, in the same way that an offer to take a lease might be. Although such a statement might not negative *animus* – because there is no inconsistency between a present intention to possess and a willingness to regularise the position if forced – such a statement, if it entails recognising the competence of the other party to grant a lawful right, could nonetheless involve acknowledgment.

16–69 In *Secretary of State for Transport v Quest Maidstone* REF/2010/0210, it was held that a query about title made with a view to purchasing the land (and acknowledging that the squatter was not the owner) – was a sufficient acknowledgment. The difference was that the query was raised not with the suspected legal owner, but with the Office of the District Valuer, a third party. Although this case turns on a question of construction, it would appear that this was a case in which the Deputy Adjudicator would have held that a conditional offer to buy, conditional upon proof of title, was a sufficient acknowledgement under s 29 of the Limitation Act 1980.

Chapter 20

Unregistered title

20–05A Pursuant to the Directive 2008/52/EC of the European Parliament and of the Council of 21 May 2008 on certain aspects of mediation in civil and commercial matters, time limits are extended under the Limitation Act 1980 – including for adverse possession – where there is cross-border mediation. In those circumstances, a time limit which would otherwise expire during the mediation is extended to as to expire after it ends.

(1) In this section—
   (a) "Mediation Directive" means Directive 2008/52/EC of the European Parliament and of the Council of 21 May 2008 on certain aspects of mediation in civil and commercial matters,
   (b) "mediation" has the meaning given by article 3(a) of the Mediation Directive,
   (c) "mediator" has the meaning given by article 3(b) of the Mediation Directive, and
   (d) "relevant dispute" means a dispute to which article 8(1) of the Mediation Directive applies (certain cross-border disputes).

(2) Subsection (3) applies where—
   (a) a time limit under this Act relates to the subject of the whole or part of a relevant dispute,
   (b) a mediation in relation to the relevant dispute starts before the time limit expires, and
   (c) if not extended by this section, the time limit would expire before the mediation ends or less than eight weeks after it ends.

(3) For the purposes of initiating judicial proceedings or arbitration, the time limit expires instead at the end of eight weeks after the mediation ends (subject to subsection (4)).

(4) If a time limit has been extended by this section, subsections (2) and (3) apply to the extended time limit as they apply to a time limit mentioned in subsection (2)(a).

(5) Where more than one time limit applies in relation to a relevant dispute, the extension by subsection (3) of one of those time limits does not affect the others.

(6) For the purposes of this section, a mediation starts on the date of the agreement to mediate that is entered into by the parties and the mediator.

(7) For the purposes of this section, a mediation ends on the date of the first of these to occur—
   (a) the parties reach an agreement in resolution of the relevant dispute,

(b) a party completes the notification of the other parties that it has withdrawn from the mediation,
(c) a party to whom a qualifying request is made fails to give a response reaching the other parties within 14 days of the request,
(d) after the parties are notified that the mediator's appointment has ended (by death, resignation or otherwise), they fail to agree within 14 days to seek to appoint a replacement mediator,
(e) the mediation otherwise comes to an end pursuant to the terms of the agreement to mediate.

(8) For the purpose of subsection (7), a qualifying request is a request by a party that another (A) confirm to all parties that A is continuing with the mediation.

(9) In the case of any relevant dispute, references in this section to a mediation are references to the mediation so far as it relates to that dispute, and references to a party are to be read accordingly.

20–05B Under the Directive, a dispute is a cross-border dispute in the following circumstances (Article 2):

1. For the purposes of this Directive a cross-border dispute shall be one in which at least one of the parties is domiciled or habitually resident in a Member State other than that of any other party on the date on which:
   (a) the parties agree to use mediation after the dispute has arisen;
   (b) mediation is ordered by a court;
   (c) an obligation to use mediation arises under national law; or
   (d) for the purposes of Article 5 an invitation is made to the parties.
2. Notwithstanding paragraph 1, for the purposes of Articles 7 and 8 a cross-border dispute shall also be one in which judicial proceedings or arbitration following mediation between the parties are initiated in a Member State other than that in which the parties were domiciled or habitually resident on the date referred to in paragraph 1(a), (b) or (c).
3. For the purposes of paragraphs 1 and 2, domicile shall be determined in accordance with Articles 59 and 60 of Regulation (EC) No 44/2001.

20–06 Add to Fn 8: See also *Wong King Lim v The Incorporated Owners of Peony House* [2013] HKCA 25 at [37].

20–28A The nature and extent of a squatter's rights were considered in *Turner v Chief Land Registrar* [2013] EWHC 1382 (Ch), at [13], Roth J held that, if a squatter who had been in possession for three years had an estate in the land at all, '... it can only be an "estate in fee simple absolute in possession". In modern parlance, that is a freehold'. At [15], he explained that: 'It is fundamental to English land law that title (at least to unregistered land) is not absolute but relative. If a squatter remains in adverse possession for 12 years, he acquires a title good against the paper owner under what is now the Limitation Act 1980, ss 15 and 17.

But in the intervening period, before the expiration of the statutory 12 years, the squatter, although he may be ejected by the owner of the paper title, is himself protected by his act of possession. He can sue strangers for trespass or nuisance and can convey the land. If he dies, the land will pass under his will or intestacy.' At [17] he said: 'Many of the authorities are helpfully gathered in the valuable work, S. Jourdan and O. Radley-Gardner, *Adverse Possession* (2nd edn, Bloomsbury Professional, 2011): see Ch 20.'

20–54 Add to Fn 86: *Kirby v Heaney* REF/2012/0608.

20–68 This paragraph was applied in *U Po Chu v Tsang Pui Ling* (DCMP 467 of 2013).

20–89A In *Turner v Chief Land Registrar* [2013] EWHC 1382 (Ch), at [19]–[20], Roth J discussed the decision in *Perry v Clissold* and concluded: '*Perry v Clissold* therefore concerned the question whether the statutory provision which entitled "the owners of the land" to compensation covered someone in the position of Mr Clissold. The Privy Council firmly rejected the Minister's contention that he was not so entitled because he was "a mere trespasser, without any estate or interest in the land". The references to the adverse possessor acquiring "an absolute title" should not be read as finding that until the expiry of the limitation period he did not hold a freehold estate, but in the same sense as the observation of Nourse L.J. quoted above, i.e. that his title then becomes impregnable as the relatively stronger title of the paper owner is then extinguished.'

Chapter 21

Registered title – Part 1

21–16 The scope of s 9 is given detailed consideration in *Sexton v Gill* REF/2013/0472/0473.

21–30 The Land Registry's practice of registering squatters on unregistered land with possessory and not absolute title was upheld in the Divisional Court in *R (Diep) v Land Registry* [2010] EWHC 3315 (Admin). The point is also discussed in *Akram v Stott* REF/2013/1088. The Law Commission propose to confirm this practice, see Law Commission CP 227 at paragraph 17.70.

21–37A In *Turner v Chief Land Registrar* [2013] EWHC 1382 (Ch), it was further held that a squatter on unregistered land with fewer than 12 years' adverse possession could also not protect his rights by caution against first registration, as this did not fall within either category of s 15(1)(a) or (b) of the Land Registration Act 2002; this is because what the squatter has is a (relative title to) freehold, and as such, it is not permissible to register a caution by reason of s 15(3)(a)(i). The Law Commission proposes a review of the general law on first registration, as set out at 2–73(4)(d)(i)–(ii) above.

21–38A Judge Rhys maintained his view in *Secretary of State for Transport v Quest Maidstone* REF/2010/0210, at [40], where, in discussion of this paragraph of the Main Work, he explained as follows:

> 'Clearly, where title to land is unregistered, different legal estates may exist concurrently – indeed, section 1(5) of the Law of Property Act 1925 expressly so provides. For example, in addition to the fee simple in possession, there may be successive leases, a rentcharge with a right of re-entry, a legal easement and a mortgage, all created in relation to the same land. To this extent, it is not right to say (as was said at paragraph 24 of *Moore v Buxton*) that there cannot be more than one legal estate in the land. However, that is not to say that different freehold estates may exist concurrently. If "freehold estate" is given its natural meaning – the fee simple absolute in possession in the land (as opposed to some lesser estate or some right in or over the land such as an easement) – it is clear that there can only be one such interest. It may be subject to defeasance – by a right of reverter, for example – but it is the sole freehold estate. Section 1(1) of the Law of Property Act 1925 provides that the only estates in land which are capable of being created or conveyed at law are (a) an estate in fee simple absolute in possession, and (b) a term of years absolute. I therefore have difficulties with the concept of two concurrently existing fee

simple absolutes in possession in the same land. Furthermore, I am not sure that the authors' analysis can assist once the title to the land has become registered.'

See also *Joslin v Hipgrave* REF/2013/942.

21–38B However, in *Sexton v Gill* REF/2013/0472/0473, Judge Rhys revisited this issue in a different context. The Respondents had secured first registration with a possessory title of a strip of land. In fact, they were not, and never had been, entitled to be so registered. The Applicants had been in adverse possession of the strip. Judge Rhys analysed the position as follows:

'[19] As far as the Respondents were concerned, they had obtained a freehold possessory title, albeit that they were not in possession. From that moment on, time did not run against them under the Limitation Act 1980. A squatter, alleging adverse possession, would be obliged to advance the claim against the Respondents under Schedule 6. That is indeed what the Applicants did. However, for as long as the Applicants remained in possession, they were also adversely possessing the land against the unregistered paper title owner. His or her estate was not registered, but is protected by the fact that the possessory title is subject to any "estate, right or interest adverse to, or in derogation of, the proprietor's title subsisting at the time of registration or then capable of arising." – see section 11(7) of the 2002 Act. If such an "estate .... adverse to, or in derogation of, the proprietor's title" remains enforceable even though its proprietor is not registered, it must follow that the estate exists outside the scheme of registration. On this basis, whilst the Limitation Act 1980 ceased to apply to the Applicants' adverse possession as against the registered proprietors – the Respondents – it had not ceased to apply to their adverse possession as against the unregistered paper title owner. On this analysis, it can be seen that the registration and subsequent "de-registration" of the Respondents does not affect in any way the Applicants' ability to bar the title of the paper title owner under the Limitation Act 1980. This being so, there is no reason in my view why the Applicants should not be entitled to be registered with a possessory title. In reaching this conclusion, I have revisited some earlier decisions of this Tribunal but am comforted to find myself agreeing with the learned editors of Jourdan & Radley-Gardner at 23–39. I would stress, however, that the present factual situation is not likely to be repeated very often.'

21–38C The Law Commission discuss this issue in CP 227 at [17.72]–[17.79], and agree with the analysis in *Sexton*. They provisionally propose that where an adverse possessor in unregistered land is registered with possessory title in the reasonable (but incorrect) belief that the prior title has been extinguished, the period of adverse possession should continue to run while the possessory title is open. An alternative analysis to that in

Sexton is that the title should simply be closed because there is another, better title that has not been extinguished.[1] If on the other hand the squatter continues in adverse possession so as to perfect his possessory title (perhaps not realising that as a result of an insolvency event the title has become vested in the Crown under the 30 year period), then it would seem unobjectionable that this should occur.

21–40 The Privy Council has had to consider the position in other jurisdictions in *Recreational Holdings 1 (Jamaica) Ltd v Lazarus (Jamaica)* [2016] UKPC 22, endorsing *Chisholm v Hall* [1959] AC 719.

21–43 The provisions are considered in helpful detail in *Blackall v Moledina* REF/2012/0865.

Reform

21–43A The Law Commission in Law Com CP 227 provisionally propose[2] the following:

> '[…] where a person becomes the first registered proprietor of title to land which has in fact been extinguished by an adverse possessor, where (i) the registered proprietor did not have notice of the adverse possessor's claim and (ii) the adverse possessor is not in actual occupation of the land at the time of registration, an application for alteration of the register should be classed as a rectification.'

21–43B This change re-balances the rights of the squatter and the 'innocent' paper title owner in a manner that was not intended by the Land Registration Act 2002. The scheme of the provision as it presently stands is that a first registered proprietor neither fixed with notice nor taking land subject to rights protected by actual occupation will defeat accrued rights on first registration. This is made clear by both the Law Com 271 at paragraph 3.47 and also in the Explanatory Notes to the 2002 Act at paragraph 41. It appears that the proposed reform in this regard is not a clarification of some deficiency in the existing drafting but a departure from the scheme as set out in the 2002 Act.

21–58 The Court of Appeal have upheld Henderson J's decision: see *Baxter v Mannion* [2011] EWCA Civ 120. The appeal concerned an application by a person who claimed to have been in adverse possession, but had not been. The failure by the paper title owner to operate the '*bureaucratic machinery*' (as the Court of Appeal described it) to object to that application resulted in the applicant becoming registered. The paper title owner claimed that this was a mistake which should be rectified. The putative squatter argued that there was no mistake on the register, that 'mistake' was technically confined to errors in procedure, and that this was not such a case. At [23]–[35], the Court of Appeal rejected the argument. It pointed out that a squatter was only entitled to apply for

1 *TFL v Al-Amini* (FTT(PC)) REF/2013/0655.

2 At paragraphs 17.49–17.62.

registration *if* he had been in adverse possession for the requisite period of ten years (Schedule 6(1)), and hence that therefore an application by a person not in relevant possession for that period was simply a bad one. It further rejected the contention that an application could not be challenged on that basis simply because the paper title owner had not objected. Finally, the Court agreed with Henderson J that it was a matter of simply justice that the title should be rectified, and that the applicant's status as proprietor in possession – as a consequence of his bad application – did not protect him ([41]–[42]). See also the general discussion of rectification in *Balevents Ltd v Sartori* [2014] EWHC 1164 (Ch), at [157]–[166].

21–61 On the occasion of an upgrading of title, the First Tier Tribunal may revisit the question of whether or not the original registration with possessory title was properly made: *Beavis v Bond* REF/2015/0043.

Chapter 22

Registered title – Part 2

22–01 An application to be registered as proprietor of a registered estate on the basis of adverse possession under Sch 6 of the 2002 Act (as opposed to defences to possession claims based on adverse possession) cannot be made to the court but only to the Land Registry: see *Swan Housing Association v Gill* [2012] EWHC 3129 (QB) and *Khan v Khan* [2015] EWHC 2625 (Ch). The Law Commission proposes to confirm that this is the only route to registration, as set out in Law Com 227 at paragraph 17.71. As to which mode of application is appropriate where an application for first registration is made, and where the squatter's 12 years have not been completed by the date of the application for registration, see the discussion by Judge Michael Mark in *Port of London v Mendoza* REF 2011/0751.

22–01A For registration in relation to encroachments by tenants, see 25–13A below.

22–16 The provisions are considered in *Morningside Residents' Association Limited v Martin* REF/2014/0193.

22–17A A new para 16 has been inserted into Sch 6, by reason of Directive 2008/52/ EC of the European Parliament and of the Council of 21 May 2008 on certain aspects of mediation in civil and commercial matters. Please refer to this Update in relation to Chapter 20. The amendment reads:

Extension of time limits because of mediation in certain cross-border disputes

(1) In this paragraph—
  (a) "Mediation Directive" means Directive 2008/52/ EC of the European Parliament and of the Council of 21 May 2008 on certain aspects of mediation in civil and commercial matters,
  (b) "mediation" has the meaning given by article 3(a) of the Mediation Directive,
  (c) "mediator" has the meaning given by article 3(b) of the Mediation Directive, and
  (d) "relevant dispute" means a dispute to which article 8(1) of the Mediation Directive applies (certain cross-border disputes).
(2) Sub-paragraph (3) applies where—
  (a) a period of time is prescribed by paragraph 1(1), 1(2)(a) or 6(1) in relation to the whole or part of a relevant dispute,
  (b) a mediation in relation to the relevant dispute starts before the period expires, and

(c) if not extended by this paragraph, the period would expire before the mediation ends or less than eight weeks after it ends.

(3) The period expires instead at the end of eight weeks after the mediation ends (subject to sub-paragraph (4)).

(4) If a period has been extended by this paragraph, sub-paragraphs (2) and (3) apply to the extended period as they apply to a period mentioned in sub-paragraph (2)(a).

(5) Where more than one period applies in relation to a relevant dispute, the extension by sub-paragraph (3) of one of those periods does not affect the others.

(6) For the purposes of this paragraph, a mediation starts on the date of the agreement to mediate that is entered into by the parties and the mediator.

(7) For the purposes of this paragraph, a mediation ends on date of the first of these to occur—

(a) the parties reach an agreement in resolution of the relevant dispute,

(b) a party completes the notification of the other parties that it has withdrawn from the mediation,

(c) a party to whom a qualifying request is made fails to give a response reaching the other parties within 14 days of the request,

(d) the parties, after being notified that the mediator's appointment has ended (by death, resignation or otherwise), fail to agree within 14 days to seek to appoint a replacement mediator,

(e) the mediation otherwise comes to an end pursuant to the terms of the agreement to mediate.

(8) For the purpose of sub-paragraph (7), a qualifying request is a request by a party that another (A) confirm to all parties that A is continuing with the mediation.

(9) In the case of any relevant dispute, references in this paragraph to a mediation are references to the mediation so far as it relates to that dispute, and references to a party are to be read accordingly.

22–29 In *Openshaw v P&F Properties Limited* REF/2013/0222, at [23]–[25], Judge Timothy Cowen said he did not think successive members of an unincorporated association could be treated as successors in title, which seems questionable. Under para 11(2)(a): 'A person is also to be regarded for those purposes as having been in adverse possession of an estate in land where he is the successor in title to an estate in the land, during any period of adverse possession by a predecessor in title to that estate'. This provision appears to have been drafted on the basis that if person A takes adverse possession of a registered estate, he will be treated as acquiring an estate in the land – an unregistered freehold estate arising by adverse possession: see Chapter 20 of the Main Work. If A then cedes that possession to person B, person B should be regarded as being the successor in title to the unregistered freehold estate arising by the adverse possession, and person B should, therefore, be able to add person A's period of possession to his own for the purposes of making up the 10 years required under Sch 6, para 1. This was the intention of the Law Commission and Land Registry, see the Final Report at [14.20]–[14.21] and [14.66].

22–39A In its Practice Guide 4, Section 3, the Land Registry say the following about Sch 6, paragraph 12:

> 'The following circumstances prevent an application being made for registration based on adverse possession
>
> [...]
>
> - the estate in land was held on trust at any time during the period of 10 years ending on the date of the application, unless the interest of each of the beneficiaries in the estate was an interest in possession (Schedule 6, paragraph 12 of the Land Registration Act 2002)
> - arguably this means that an application cannot be made where, at any point [*during this period, the registered proprietor at the time (i) was dead and their estate was being administered, (ii) was bankrupt and their property was being administered by the trustee in bankruptcy or (iii) (being a company) was being wound up. In each of these cases the registered estate is subject to a form of trust (Ayerst v C & K (Construction) Ltd [1976] A.C. 167)*]'

22–39B It is questionable whether the argument referred to there, based on the *Ayerst* case is correct. In *Ayerst*, the issue was whether shares were in the 'beneficial ownership' of a company which was the subject of a winding-up order. The House of Lords held that they were not, because the assets of a company being wound up could not be used for the benefit of the company. Lord Diplock said that there was no 'trust' in the strict sense of the word recognised by equity, because there were no identifiable beneficiaries. However, he said: '*It is no misuse of language to describe the property as being held by the trustee on a statutory trust if the qualifying adjective "statutory" is understood as indicating that the trust does not bear all the indicia which characterise a trust as it was recognised by the Court of Chancery apart from statute.*' [There is nothing in the Joint Report to suggest that Sch 6, para 12 was intended to apply to a situation such as that in *Ayerst* where there is no 'trust' in the strict sense of the word recognised by equity, and no possibility of a reversionary interest. The language of para 12 suggests that the intention was that it should only apply to trusts with beneficiaries. That is supported by *Best v Curtis* REF/2015/0130 at [24]: 'Paragraph 12 assumes a trust that has beneficiaries'.]

22–57A In *Hopkins v Beacon & Beacon* [2011] EWHC 2899 (Ch), Vos J decided that an objection by the paper title owner, but failing additionally to tick the box on the NAP requiring the case to be dealt with under Sch 6, para 5, did not automatically bar the paper title owner from subsequently asking for the application to be so treated. However, it had to be clear from the contents of the NAP that paragraph 5 was being invoked: '*....the form NAP in this case must be such that a reasonable* *registrar would have been left in no reasonable doubt that it was a notice invoking paragraph 5.*' On the facts of *Hopkins*, the form was not clear enough.[1] A similar argument failed in *CalonYnTyfuCyfyngedig v Robert Martyn John Hutton* (Adverse possession) [2012] EWLandRA 2011_0722 (before Deputy Adjudicator Owen Rhys), and also in *King v Suffolk County Council* REF/2015/0867 (before Judge Ann McAllister). An example of the paper title owner succeeding is *Norton Arms Bowls Club v Spirit Pub Company (Leased) Limited* (Adverse possession) [2013] EWLandRA 2013_0318 (before Judge Robert Abbey).

22–60 There is no power to extend the 65 business day time limit: *Fontaine v Bertolussi* REF/2010/0499.

22–64 Please refer further to *Hopkins v Beacon & Beacon* [2011] EWHC 2899 (Ch), at paragraph 22–57A above.

22–75 For an application of the estoppel ground, see *Tomlinson v Foster* REF/2011/1049 at [76].

22–79 It remains the case in practice that the ground is encountered where the squatter has been in adverse possession of land for 12 years whilst that land was unregistered and before the squatter was able to vindicate his claim to title to the land, the land became registered. In those circumstances, the application would be made while the land was registered, and therefore any application for registration would be on the basis of registered land: see *Cooper and Cooper v Gick* REF/2007/0103 and *Pawson v Vanes* REF/2015/0339; 0340.

22–80 As is noted by Deputy Adjudicator McAllister in *Crosdil v Hodder* REF/2009/1177, where reliance on the second condition failed, it is difficult to envisage a case in which this ground will be of assistance to an applicant, as typically the applicant will have a remedy other than one based on adverse possession: see at [26]–[31]. The Law Commission will be revisiting this issue in its proposed review of the 2002 Act: see 2–73(4) above.

22–86 Contrary to the view expressed in the Second Edition of the Main Work in footnote 92, the Court of Appeal has twice assumed that the reasonable belief under Sch 6, para 5(4) must be held up to the date of the application by the squatter:

(1) In *Zarb v Parry* [2011] EWCA Civ 1306, Arden LJ stated that:

> '[54] As this is the first decision of this court about the operation of section 98 of, and paragraph 5(4) of schedule 6 to, the 2002 Act, I will conclude with some observations on the way in which the new provisions operate.
>
> [55] The 2002 Act creates difficulties for proprietors with disputed boundaries. If a person discovers that his boundary is in fact on

1 See at [51], [63]. The insufficiently clear statement is set out in paragraph 11 of the judgment. It was the following: 'If Mr & Mrs Beacon believed the land was theirs, why did they not query their land registry title when it was issued in March 2002?? Or any other ordinance or boundary plan??'.

his neighbour's land and that he has been in possession for ten years, he can if he acts promptly apply to the Land Registry to be registered as proprietor of any land outside his title. The new provisions will, however, require the registrar to give notice of the application to the paper title owner of the land sought to be acquired. If the registered proprietor does not oppose the application, registration will follow. If the registered proprietor opposes the application, the adverse possessor may be unable to satisfy the third condition in paragraph 5 of schedule 6 to the 2002 Act, and will fail to secure registration save in the exceptional case where he can show that another condition is satisfied.

[56] In the present case, the Zarbs wished to sidestep the need for legal proceedings for possession of the Strip by dispossessing the Parrys. They were, on the law as I have held it to be and the facts as found by the judge, unsuccessful. They also took proceedings which had the result that the Parrys could not make any application for registration of the Strip in their own names. The result of the judge's findings, however, is that the Zarbs' paper title has been lost by the operation of section 98 of the 2002 Act.

[57] If, however, the Parrys had been away on holiday when the Zarbs tried to dispossess them from the Strip, the Zarbs might well have completed the act of dispossession. In those circumstances, the Parrys would on these facts have been able to secure registration of the Strip in their own name if they had made an application for registration within six months. They could have added together their occupation of the land with that of the Ceens. There would have been no need meanwhile for the Parrys to take down the Zarb's newly-erected boundary fence and re-establish their possession of the Strip while that matter was being dealt with by the Land Registry. But, if the application is not made within six months, the adverse possessor may be unable to satisfy the conditions in paragraph 5 of schedule 6.'

(2) The same assumption was made in *Iam Group Plc v Chowdrey* [2012] EWCA Civ 505, at [4] and [15].

22–86A The point was not argued in either case, and the decision did not in any event turn on that issue as in both cases the belief was established to the date of the application or possession proceedings. It is therefore considered that neither case is to be treated as authoritatively settling the point.[1] Adjudicator and First Tier Tribunal decisions have expressed a range of views on the issue. The issue was left open in *Griffin*

1 The ratio decidendi of a case is any rule of law expressly or impliedly treated by the judge as a necessary step in reaching his conclusion, having regard to the line of reasoning adopted by him. To follow the line of reasoning, one must start with the issue the court had to decide: *Deane v Secretary of State for Work and Pensions* [2011] 1 WLR 743 at [32]–[33]. Given that the point was not argued, and made no difference to the outcome, the observations on it were not part of the ratio in either case.

v Crown Mill (1993) Management Ltd [2015] EWLandRA 2014_0941 (Judge McAllister). Arden LJ's views in *Zarb* were given critical consideration by Judge Mark in *Port of London Authority v Paul Mendoza* [2016] EWLandRA 2011_0751. Those views were treated as binding by Deputy Adjudicator Rhys in *Tomlinson v Foster* [2012] EWLandRA 2011_1049, but the contrary was not argued. In *McLeod v Brown and Jones* REF/2013/0833 Judge Green held that, although the belief must have been had during the period of adverse possession, and must have been held for at least 10 years, it did not have to be established as continuing up to the date of the application. However, he did not refer to *Zarb*.

Commentator opinion is equally divided. In '"Reasonable belief" in adverse possession' Estates Gazette 30 May 2015, S Tozer and K Lees argue that *Zarb* was right on this point. On the other hand P. Milne, 'Mistaken belief and adverse possession – mistaken interpretation? *IAM Group plc v Chowdrey*' [2012] Conveyancer 342, written by a solicitor at the Land Registry, argues it was wrong. The controversy is usefully discussed in Law Com 227, at paragraph 17.38.

There appear to be three possible views:

(1) That the reasonable belief must be held up to the date on which the application is made (ie, a form of 'next before action' as under the Prescription Act 1832); or
(2) There is implicit a grace period whereby the falsification of a subjective belief hitherto reasonable does not preclude an application provided that the squatter acts promptly, or within a reasonable time of ceasing to hold the belief or of the belief ceasing to be reasonable; or
(3) That it is sufficient that the squatter has, by the time of the application, had a ten-year period of holding a reasonable belief, whether or not he was disabused of that belief before the application was made. This appears to have been what Law Com 271, para 14.44 had in mind.

22–86B The Law Commission will be revisiting this issue in its proposed review of the 2002 Act: see 2–73(4) above and, in more detail, paragraph 22–118 below.

22–86C It is established by both *Zarb* and *IAM* that the mere fact that a belief has been challenged does not render it unreasonable to hold that belief. This was stated in *IAM* at [29]:

> 'So far as concerns the letters from the appellant challenging the title of the respondent to the disputed property in 2009 and 2010, it is clear from *Zarb v Parry* that the mere fact that a paper title owner challenges the asserted ownership of land by the adverse possessor is not in every case sufficient to render unreasonable any continuing belief of ownership on the part of adverse possessor. On the facts in *Zarb v Parry* the adverse possessor satisfied the requirement of reasonable belief even though that the paper title owner had challenged the assertion of ownership by the adverse possessor.'

22–86D Further, the Court of Appeal in *IAM* decided as follows as to the person whose belief had to be tested (at [27]):

> '... the issue is not the knowledge of a reasonably competent solicitor acting for the `respondent in 1993. We are not here concerned with knowledge in the context, which frequently arises, of imputing an agent's knowledge to the principal. We are here concerned with the requirement as to the reasonable belief of a particular person. In this case, it is the respondent, but generally it is the person who is seeking to apply for registration of title by virtue of adverse possession. What is in issue therefore is not imputed knowledge but rather whether that particular person – here the respondent – was reasonable in holding the belief that he or she did in all the circumstances.'

In the same vein, see *Crosdil v Hodder* REF/2009/1177; *Osborne v Lawton* REF/2010/1066; *McLeod v Brown* REF/2013/0833.

22–91A Where a squatter's application has been referred to the Adjudicator, is then struck out for non-compliance and removed from the Day List and then subsequently reinstated on appeal, is the application to be reinstated on the Day List as if it had never been struck out (ie restored retrospectively), or is it to take effect from the date of the order allowing the appeal? The issue came before the Court of Appeal in *Chief Land Registrar v Franks* [2011] EWCA Civ 772. The Court of Appeal agreed with the judgment of Briggs J below, that the Court had jurisdiction to make a retrospective restoration order. However, a distinction had to be drawn between (a) 'no third party interest cases', that is, cases where there were no subsequent dealings with the land which retrospective restoration would interfere with, and (b) 'third party interest cases', where such interests did exist. Arden LJ said as follows about those two classes of cases:

> '[48] In [...] a "no third party interest" case, I can see no reason why the court would not have jurisdiction to make a restoration order. I should add, however, that it may be that the time for inquiry as to whether any such interest has in the meantime arisen is not only when the court makes its order but also at the later stage when the registrar comes to give effect to it. That, however, would require only a minor adjustment to the procedure: the restoration order might have to provide for a reference back to the court if in the meantime a third party interest had arisen.
>
> [49] Subject to that consideration, I would regard it as plain that in a "no third party interest" case the court does have jurisdiction to make a restoration order. Its making would not have any effect on the Act's scheme of priority; and, in the ordinary course, I can see no reason why the court should not make such an order. On the contrary, I can see good reason why it should do so. Such an order would achieve a real "as you were" position that ought to be a proper objective of the court in disposing of the appeal; and it would enable the original application to be disposed of just as, but for the adjudicator's error, it ought to have been disposed of.

It would, on the face of it, therefore be the correct order to make [...].

[51] In my judgment, if, as I consider, the court has jurisdiction in a "no third party interest" case to make a restoration order, it must follow that it also has jurisdiction to make a restoration order in a "third party interest" case such as that before Briggs J. There can be no logical basis for the proposition that, once third party interests have intervened, the jurisdiction disappears. The only question that circumstances such as that will provoke is whether or not the jurisdiction should be exercised; and, if yes, on what, if any, terms and conditions.

[...]

[53] I ought not to part with this appeal without adding that, having so ruled against the registrar, I recognise the force of Mr Morshead's submissions that an exercise of the jurisdiction to make a restoration order in a "third party interest" case will in principle impair the integrity of the Act's scheme as to priority. I regard the submissions as very powerful. It appears to me to follow from his argument that, if, as I consider, the court has jurisdiction to make a restoration order, it ought not ordinarily to exercise it in a "third party interest" case since it cannot ordinarily be a proper exercise of the court's jurisdiction to make an order whose effect is to re-arrange the scheme of priorities provided for by the Act.

[54] In the light of the way the appeal was argued, I propose, however, to say no more on that save to add that, in the previous paragraph, I twice used the word "ordinarily" and did so because I do not wish to be taken as suggesting that in every 'third party interest' case there will be only one way in which the jurisdiction could properly be exercised. Trite though it is, "never say never" remains, in my view, a wise piece of judicial caution.'

22–99 In *Gill v McCarthy* REF/2014/0495/0661/0838, it was made clear that Sch 6, para 6 was only of application if an application under the 2002 Act was rejected because the squatter was required to, but could not make out, one of the grounds under Sch 6, para 5. It did not apply where the application was rejected or cancelled for some other reason. The Law Commission proposes that this issue should be examined and clarified: see 2–73(4) above.

Reform: Law Commission CP 227

22–109 The Law Commission proposes changes to the Sch 6 machinery in CP 227, as already indicated in Chapter 2, above. Whilst a wholesale reform of the Sch 6 procedure is not proposed, the areas of concern have been identified by the Law Commission which require consideration following the consultation process are as follows:

(1) Whether more than one application can be made under Sch 6;
(2) Whether the Third Condition (reasonable mistake as to boundary) under Sch 6, para 5, requires reconsideration and whether the first two conditions serve any purpose.

Multiple Applications

22–110 The Law Commission is proposing to clarify the position of an applicant squatter whose application has been rejected, and whether a second application can be made by the same squatter in those circumstances.

22–111 It is necessary to distinguish between two forms of rejection:

(1) The Law Commission notes that a first application may be rejected without the registered proprietor being notified because, for instance, the relevant fee has not been paid, or there is no evidence of adverse possession, or there is no evidence of possession for ten years.[1]
(2) Alternatively, the application may be rejected following notification to the registered proprietor (or other person who has been served) on the basis of a counter-notice given by the proprietor, and if the three conditions under Sch 6, para 5 are not met. This rejection occurs under para 6 of Sch 6. It is the current practice of the Land Registry not to allow a second application in such a case. Instead, the squatter will only succeed if he has been in possession for two further years.[2]

22–112 The proposal of the Law Commission is that,[3] if the application is rejected under para 6 of Sch 6, then the squatter cannot make a second application based on ten years but must instead wait and see if the registered proprietor vindicates his title within the further two year period. If, on the other hand, the application is simply rejected by the Land Registry prior to notification, then the Law Commission take the view that, subject to consultation, the squatter ought to be able to try again. It is considered that this is sensible and conforms with the scheme of the 2002 Act.

The Schedule 6, paragraph 5 Conditions

22–113 The proposals of the Law Commission here are potentially more radical.[4] It will be recalled that under the existing scheme, a squatter can only succeed in the face of a counter-notice if one of three conditions is met under Sch 6, para 5. These have been discussed in the Main Work at paragraphs 22–72 and following, and in this Update. In essence, the first condition is that the squatter can rely on an estoppel, the second is that there is 'some other reason' to be registered, and the third is that there is a reasonable mistake as to the boundary between the properties.

1 At para. 17.17.
2 At 17.18; the two year period is of course provided for in Sch 6, para 6 itself.
3 Law Com CP 227 at 17.24.
4 Law Com CP 227 at 17.25.

The First and Second Conditions

22–114 In relation to the first and second conditions, the Law Commission considers there is a case that they should be removed from Sch 6 (subject to evidence of any use of those conditions which emerges from the consultation process).

22–115 The first condition, based on estoppel, is arguably superfluous. In order to invoke the jurisdiction, the squatter has to demonstrate that he was in adverse possession. However, if he is compelled to invoke the first condition, then the squatter will only succeed if he establishes an estoppel, and can further establish that it gives rise to an equity which can only be satisfied by conferral of title to the land he has been in possession of. Aside from acting as a gateway into the Tribunal's jurisdiction to determine the estoppel, adverse possession therefore adds nothing.[1] This kind of case may be dealt with more efficiently by simply giving the Tribunal an enhanced jurisdiction to deal with pure estoppel claims.[2]

22–116 The second condition, 'some other reason' to be registered, is unclear in function, though the Law Commission Report, Law Com 271, which gave rise to the 2002 Act scheme gives two examples where a squatter might succeed: in the event that the squatter is entitled to the land in question under the will of the registered proprietor, or by intestate succession, or in the event that the squatter is entitled to the land under an uncompleted sale contract, so that he is the beneficiary under a bare trust.[3]

22–117 In practice, the second condition is hardly used at all, and, if used, is either used to found unmeritorious claims to be registered for bad reasons, or it is used where the squatter has mistakenly invoked the Sch 6 procedure when he could have succeeded under the pre-2002 Act law. The Law Commission proposes that, were the second condition to be removed, the latter basis for securing registration would be preserved.[4]

The Third Condition

22–118 As discussed above at 22–86 and following, and in the Main Work, paragraphs 22–85 to 22–91, this is both the most practically significant condition and the one in respect of which most difficulty has arisen in the cases and commentary. The Law Commission propose that the third condition should be amended, so that the squatter is required to apply under Sch 6 within six months of his reasonable belief coming to an end. It is noted at paragraph 17.47 of Law Com CP 227 that it may be more difficult to establish when the reasonable belief has come to an end, and what therefore is a sufficient 'trigger' for ending that

1 And may in any event not arise, as the inchoate equity that the putative squatter has in such a case might itself furnish a right to occupy, rendering his use lawful.
2 As is considered in Chapter 21 of Law Com CP 227.
3 Law Commission, Law Com 271, paragraph 14.43.
4 Law Commission, Law Com 227, paragraph 17.35.

belief. It is considered (as discussed above in paragraph 22–86A) that it is preferable to clarify the third condition to require the squatter to prove ten years' reasonable belief ending at any time. It is considered that to require those who have made reasonable mistakes as to their boundaries to rush to Tribunal proceedings (which are beginning to resemble ever more closely county court proceedings) is contrary to the general view of the courts that boundary disputes are to be discouraged, wherever possible.[1]

1 And see the comments of C Harpum at paragraphs 161 and following in his consultation response: http://www.falcon-chambers.com/images/uploads/articles/Response_to_LC_CP_227_on_Land_Registration_%282%29.pdf

Chapter 23

Easements, profits and other rights

23–02 The same is true in relation to rights of common: *Mellstrom v Badgworthy Land Company Limited* REF/2008/1498, 2009/0290, 2009/0953. Whilst the ownership of the land in the commons register might change by reason of successful adverse possession, the rights of the commoners under the scheme are unaffected.

23–29 The cases cited in this paragraph are discussed in *Harepath LLP v Care and Skill Pest Control Limited* REF/2015/0156.

Chapter 24

Leases

24–22 This is further illustrated by the unusual facts in *Mitchell v Watkinson* [2014] EWCA Civ 1472. A father gifted his son some fields. After the gift (when he no longer owned the land) the father granted a written lease of the same fields to three individuals who were the trustees of a cricket club. This created a tenancy by estoppel, binding as between the father and the trustees. The members of the club, licensed by the trustees, then went about the business of the club. The trustees were then directed to pay rent to the son, which they did. This created an implied periodic tenancy between the son and the trustees on the terms of the written tenancy agreement. The trustees subsequently stopped paying rent. The Court of Appeal, agreeing with Morgan J, decided that there was no 'lease in writing' between the son and the club trustees, and that the club trustees were therefore in adverse possession via their licensees, the club members, following the last payment of rent.

24–37 This passage was cited with approval by Morgan J at first instance in *Mitchell v Watkinson* [2013] EWHC 2266 (Ch), at [52] and following. It was not discussed on appeal ([2014] EWCA Civ 1472).

24–47 At Fn 9: add *Khan v Khan* [2015] EWHC 2625 (Ch).

Chapter 25

Encroachments

25–1A The law relating to tenant's encroachments has proven a fertile source of cases and comment since the Second Edition of the Main Work. Of principal importance is a very important decision of the Hong Kong Court of Final Appeal, *Secretary of Justice v Chau Ka Chik Tso* [2011] HKCFA 86 in which there was a division of opinion, split three to two, as to whether and to what extent limitation plays any role in the doctrine of encroachment at all. Whilst the division of opinion was of mainly academic interest to the outcome of that appeal, it is of real interest in practical terms.

25–1B If not a creature of limitation, and not a species of adverse possession, then tenant encroachment-based claims do *not* fall to be decided under the Limitation Act 1980 (and hence such principles as acknowledgment, the rules relating to adverse possession and leases, and so on do not apply), or under Sch 6 to the Land Registration Act 2002, so that the statutory machinery for resolving adverse possession claims, and the limitations placed upon such claims, are also inapplicable.

Basis of Encroachment: The Options

25–1C In her survey of the law,[1] Dr Lees has suggested that there are really only three options as to how encroachment could be classified in English law:

> '(1) Encroachment, although based on possession, is not based on adverse possession. Thus, section 8 excludes the operation of section 15, and so section 96 and 97 LRA 2002 do not apply, and as such encroachment operates entirely without Schedule 6. A tenant would then rely on Sch 4, para 2(1)(b) to bring the register up to date.
>
> (2) Encroachment is based on adverse possession albeit a modified version and the Limitation Act does apply. Then the tenant could apply under Schedule 6, and the provisions of that will determine whether the application is successful or not. If the landlord were to serve a counter- notice, the tenant may be able to bring him or herself into the protection of the boundary exception, dependant upon the interpretation of "belonging to".

1 E Lees, 'Encroachments and Schedule 6 LRA 2002: unknotting the tangle' (2015) Conveyancer and Property Lawyer 110.

(3) Encroachment can be based on adverse possession where there is no consent of the landlord, in which case the tenant can apply under Schedule 6. In this case, if the situation is based on a combination of estoppel and adverse possession, then he may be able to rely on the equity arising by estoppel for the purposes of paragraph 5.'

The Outcome in Chau Ka Chik Tso

25–1D Which of those options is correct depends on the true characterisation of encroachment. In *Ka Chik Tso* it was assumed that the doctrine of encroachment was applicable to the facts. The question for the court was whether this amounted to adverse possession and whether it mattered that the tenant relying on encroachment had occupied under two sequential leases, one replacing the other and whether his encroachment rights benefited him under his second lease. On the first question, the nature of encroachment, the five judge court was split 2:3 as to reasons, but unanimous in outcome.

25–1E In essence, the differences in view can be expressed as follows: the minority was of the view that the landlord and tenant relationship gave rise to a presumption that the tenant, if encroaching, was doing so under his lease and would be estopped from denying that this was so. Limitation played no direct role in that interpretation, save that the landlord (or third party) might find his right of recovery barred for the duration of the lease during which period the estoppel operated. For the majority, the doctrine worked as a true form of adverse possession, albeit vesting in the squatter a leasehold and not a freehold, interest and not barring the title of the person against whom adverse possession was occurring.

25–1F The minority reasons were given by Mr Justice Ribiero PJ, with whom Mr Justice Chan PJ agreed. The core of his reasons are at [40]–[41], and [64]–[65]:

'40. In my view, Willes J's decision [*a reference to Whitmore v Humphries*] suggests a way out of the doctrinal difficulties mentioned above. But for intervention of the doctrine, an encroaching tenant who has occupied the land encroached upon for longer than the limitation period might well be able factually to set up adverse possession as the basis for both barring his landlord's right of action to recover the land and extinguishing his landlord's title to it. However, the doctrine gives the landlord some protection by presuming that the tenant's occupation of the encroachment area is as an annex to his demised holding and estopping the tenant from contending that his possession is adverse to his landlord.

41. The limitation period is still important since the doctrine is only needed and only comes into play to defeat a potential plea of adverse possession barring the landlord's right of action after the period has run out. However, the doctrine does not

incorporate as an ingredient the operation of any provisions of the Limitation Ordinance to bar the landlords right of action. It is not the law of limitation, but the combined effect of the presumption and the estoppel arising under the doctrine, that converts the tenant's occupation in such circumstances into a leasehold interest in the encroachment area. After the prescribed statutory period, the presumption equally applies to the landlord who benefits from the doctrine so that he is deemed to have granted the tenant a leasehold interest over the land encroached upon on the same terms as the existing tenancy. It is for that reason, and not because his right of action has been extinguished as against a trespasser, that the landlord cannot recover possession of the area of encroachment until the lease comes to an end.

[...]

64. In my view, the authorities discussed above show that in cases involving encroachment on the landlord's land, the doctrine operates by giving effect to the presumption and the estoppel discussed above. If the limitation period has not yet expired, the tenant may of course be ejected and cannot plead the Limitation Ordinance to meet the landlord's claim. However, upon expiry of the limitation period, the doctrine comes into play and the Limitation Ordinance would still not provide a defence to the landlord's claim. This is because the doctrine operates so that the tenant is presumed to have occupied the encroachment on the same terms as apply to his demised holding and he is estopped from asserting that he was, on the contrary, in adverse possession. In such cases, the presumption applies equally to the landlord. The doctrine protects his interest from being destroyed by operation of the Limitation Ordinance but the price extracted by the law for such protection is that the landlord must accept that the tenant has acquired a leasehold interest over the encroachment, with possession to be recovered by the landlord only after determination of the lease.

65. In the present case, it is common ground that the presumption that the respondents held the additional land as part of the demised holding has not been rebutted. It is also common ground that they have occupied such land continuously since at least 1924. It follows that the 60 year limitation period applicable to Government claims to recover land expired in 1984, when, subject to the effect (if any) of the Renewal Ordinance, the doctrine took effect, estopping the respondents from asserting, contrary to the presumption, that they have, by adverse possession, acquired a possessory title and extinguished the Government's title. Since the presumption applies equally to the Government (subject to the Renewal Ordinance) it became bound to accept that the respondents had acquired a leasehold interest in the additional land on the terms of their Government leases, expiring at the end of their term.'

25–1G The effect of that reasoning is therefore that the estoppel and presumption mean that the tenant is simply unable to invoke limitation periods, which have nothing directly to do with the position save indirectly as follows: the tenant can be evicted before the limitation period expires, but afterwards, the landlord cannot evict the tenant but the tenant is estopped from denying his landlord's title and that the basis of his occupation is as tenant.[1]

25–1H Lord Scott of Foscote NPJ (with whom Mr Justice Bokhary PJ and Mr Justice Litton NPJ agreed) reached the same result by a different route. In his opinion, the use by the encroaching tenant was in each case adverse possession in the limitation sense. His core reasoning was as follows:

> '108. The principle of "encroachment" is that if a tenant goes into, and remains in, occupation of land belonging to his landlord, it is to be presumed, particularly if the encroached-upon land is adjoining the demised land, that the tenant's encroachment is intended by him to annex the encroached-upon land to his demised land so as to enable him to occupy and use the encroached-upon land as if it were part and parcel of the demised land (see *Kingsmill v Millard* (1855) 11 Exch 313 at 318). The presumption, although imposed by judge-made law, is a rebuttable one and can be rebutted by evidence that the tenant intended to occupy the encroached-upon land not simply as tenant but as owner.
>
> 109. It is not in dispute that this presumption does apply to the encroachment by the plaintiffs, or by their respective predecessors-in-title, on to the parts of the 6.67 acres adjoining their respective sections. Nor is it in dispute that the presumption has not been rebutted. The plaintiffs, it follows, are bound to accept that they, and their predecessors, have occupied their respective parts of the 6.67 acres as annexes to their demised land and on the same terms as those on which they hold their demised land under their leases. But the oddity, or one of the oddities, of the encroachment presumption is that it is unilateral. It binds the encroaching lessee, unless rebutted, but it does not bind the lessor until, either, by his conduct or by the nature of his acquiescence he accepts the presumption, or, by the expiry of the relevant limitation period, he becomes unable to recover possession of the encroached-upon land and must, perforce, accept the presumption.
>
> 110. This feature of the presumption, namely, that it does not, and cannot, initially at least, bind the landlord, the owner of the encroached-upon land, is important. It follows that the landlord can, so long as he is not bound by the presumption, treat the encroacher, his tenant of the demised land, as a trespasser on the encroached-upon land and obtain against him all or any of the

1 This is perhaps more in line with the view expressed in *Skipwith v Singh* REF/2009/850 at paragraphs 10 and 12.

remedies that the law allows against a trespasser. These remedies include an order ejecting the encroacher from the encroached-upon land, an injunction against re-entry, payment of mesne profits and damages for trespass.

111. It seems to me to follow, also, that so long as the landlord, the owner of the encroached-upon land, remains entitled to treat the encroacher, his tenant of the demised land, as a trespasser vis-a-vis the encroached-upon land, it cannot be denied that the trespasser's possession of the encroached-upon land is "adverse" to the landlord for limitation purposes. And it follows from this that if the owner of the encroached-upon land does nothing, whether through inertia or through ignorance of the encroachment is immaterial, time for limitation purposes may run and if the limitation period expires the landlord will lose the right to treat the encroacher as a trespasser and will no longer be able to seek an order ejecting the trespasser from the encroached-upon land. On the expiry of the limitation period the encroacher will no longer be a trespasser and will be able, for the time being at least, to resist an order for possession sought by the landlord.

112. But the effect of the encroaching trespasser's adverse possession is, as it seems to me, necessarily limited by the unrebutted presumption. The encroacher's presumed intention is to occupy the land in question as an annex to his or her demised land. The encroacher will, therefore, on the termination of the demise of the demised land, be under an obligation to deliver up to the landlord not only the demised land but also the encroached-upon land held as an annex to the demised land. To that extent, therefore, the encroacher's possession of the encroached-upon land has not been adverse to the landlord. It seems to me, as a matter of principle, that the effect of a trespasser's possession must depend upon the trespasser's intentions. If the trespasser's intentions are to take possession of the land in a capacity not that of full ownership but limited in some way, then it seems to me that the consequences of that possession, if it has continued for the requisite limitation period, should, in principle, be limited accordingly. It should be no part of the function of statutes of limitation to give long enjoyed possession of land a consequence never intended by the possessor. I know of no authority to the contrary.

113. I conclude, therefore, that if a lessee enters into and remains in possession of land belonging to his lessor and adjoining the demised land and does so with the intention, presumed and unrebutted or simply proved, of thereby enlarging the demised land and treating the encroached-upon land as annexed to the demised land, his (the lessee's) possession is adverse possession, for he is in complete and exclusive possession and is, unless the lessor has consented to the encroachment, undoubtedly a trespasser. But it is a limited adverse possession, for it does not deny, and indeed accepts, the right of the lessor, the owner,

to recover possession on the termination of the demise. It is adverse only for the limited purpose of acquiring a title during the continued currency of the demise. In such a case, there is, in my opinion, no reason why, if the possession continues uninterrupted for the requisite limitation period, the encroacher should not obtain, in effect, a leasehold title to the encroached-upon land for a period commensurate with the term for which he holds the demised land, and every reason why, on the expiry of that term, the lessor should be entitled to recover possession not only of the demised land but also of the encroached-upon land. Section 9(1) of the Limitation Ordinance would, in my opinion, apply.'

25–1I The effect of this reasoning is, therefore, (i) that the tenant does generate a proprietary interest through his possession, which is adverse to the relevant paper title, but (ii) that the nature of that interest is limited by reference to the intention ascribed to him by presumption. If he intends to hold as tenant, he will hold an interest which corresponds with that intention, that is, a leasehold interest.

25–1J Whilst there is something to be said for the historical basis of the minority view, the reasoning of Lord Scott NPJ appears to sit most comfortably with the modern law of adverse possession. It is difficult to see why a tenant should not face the same limitation period hurdles as any other squatter. That said, there are potential doctrinal difficulties with the majority view, particularly in relation to unregistered land:

(1) First of all, it appears to ascribe to adverse possession a wholly 'positive' function, that is, it appears to suggest that, like prescription, it is a way of 'growing' a new right, in the form of an addition to the demise. However, adverse possession in the original sense is negative in effect, in that it operates to bar actions, leaving the rights of the squatter as the only rights standing.
(2) Secondly, and on a related note, it is not the case that under adverse possession a squatter can somehow choose what right he has by reference to his intentions. The majority's suggestion in *Chau Ka Chik Tso* that this might be so when a tenant is a lessee is inconsistent with those cases where the squatter has a mistaken belief that he has a tenancy,[1] which do not produce the same effect, and sit uncomfortably with cases of adverse possession against land subject to leasehold interests, at least where that land is unregistered.[2]
(3) Thirdly, it is difficult to see how encroachment by a squatting tenant against land extinguishes anything, as is required by the statutory

1 Main Work at 9–44. To that extent we would differ with the analysis of Dr Lees in relation to requisite intention expressed at p 116. We do not consider that a genuine subjective intention to hold land as part of an extended demise for one's own benefit and for the benefit of a landlord is inconsistent with the *animus possidendi* presumed from conduct.

2 For the position on leases, see Chapters 19–22 of the Main Work.

language of the Limitation Act 1980 (*...the title of that person to the land shall be extinguished*, s 17(1)).[1]

(4) Fourthly, even if it can be said that encroachment entails adverse possession so as to trigger the Sch 6 procedure under the 2002 Act, encroachment is a poor fit with the exceptions which can be invoked by an ordinary squatter under Sch 6:

   (a) The first condition under Schedule 6 paragraph 5(2) (the 'estoppel ground') requires there to be an estoppel making it unconscionable for the registered proprietor to dispossess the tenant. However, it is doubtful that encroachment entails an estoppel operating on the registered proprietor, as it rather appears to be either a procedural or a substantive estoppel precluding the tenant, that is, the putative squatter, from asserting a claim to a freehold title. Further, it would seem from s 110(4) (conferring on the Adjudicator jurisdiction to deal with estoppels) that the estoppel the first condition has in mind is a proprietary estoppel (see also paragraph 22–75 of the Main Work, and Law Com 271 at 14.40). Whatever the nature of the estoppel in an encroachment case, it is, despite the potential for factual overlap, a proprietary estoppel.

   (b) The second condition is that the squatter is for some other reason entitled to be registered as proprietor of 'the estate'. The looseness of 'other reason' may appear to assist, but it is clear that the reference to 'the estate' is a reference to the estate of the dispossessed registered proprietor. However 'all' the squatter is entitled to get in an encroachment case is a leasehold, which is not an estate which is formerly vested in the registered proprietor but rather an estate generated anew by the putative squatter. Again, the drafting appears to preclude encroachment.

   (c) The third condition – general boundaries – will of course only help if (a) the lease is registered (otherwise there are no general boundaries) and (b) if there is land 'belonging' to the applicant if a tenant is 'all' he is, and (c) if the land is adjacent (and we know that the doctrine applies to non-contiguous land), and (d) it is possible to maintain a reasonable belief about a boundary if one has extended one's paper title boundary by means of encroachment.

25–1K Were the minority reasoning to be accepted (as Dr Lees contends it should), the law would be as follows:

(1) Where T has encroached on L's land, that is not 'adverse possession' in the sense of either the Limitation Act 1980 or the Land Registration Act 2002. Instead, after the expiry of the limitation period, it would be possible for the encroaching tenant to apply

1 The extinctive effect of section 17 is of course expressly disapplied in relation to registered land governed by the 2002 Act (s 96(3)).

to update the register to reflect his extended demise under Sch 4, para 2(1)(b) (assuming that the lease is registered).

(2) If T has encroached on land belonging to L, and wishes to formalise his position by updating his title to reflect that position, then that would (in the case of registered leases) be an alteration under Sch 4 of the 2002 Act or, as the Land Registry suggest, an application for first registration.[1] L does not have the benefit or constraints of Sch 6 of the 2002 Act.

(3) There is nothing to bar a claim by L against a third party using T's possession, however. This is not directly to do with encroachment, but rather 'traditional' adverse possession. In support of this, it might be said that there is no real analytical difference between L taking advantage of encroachment onto X's land by T pursuant to an existing lease, and adverse possession by the squatter granting a lease over land, which has been held to amount to an act of possession.[2] Under the LRA 2002, L would need, somehow, to establish one of the three conditions that are in place, which would, it is submitted, be difficult to do.

25–1L It is far from clear whether the English courts will follow the minority or the majority judgments in *Chau Ka Chik Tso*. There are strong arguments in favour of both. The minority approach is more in keeping with the historical development of the encroachment principle, while the majority approach appears to restore principle to an area of law that has developed in an unprincipled manner. It will be for the courts to decide the outcome, as the Law Commission decided not to investigate this issue in full in Law Com CP 227: see 17.81. The Law Commission's only proposal in relation to encroachments was that, where a tenant is in adverse possession of land (other than land belonging to the landlord) and the presumption that the tenant is acting on behalf of his or her landlord is not rebutted, the landlord should be able to make an application under Sch 6 based on the tenant's adverse possession: 17.86.

25–01 The principles as between a tenant and land belonging to a third party were set out conveniently by Morgan J at paragraph [83] of *Balevents Ltd v Sartori* [2014] EWHC 1164 (Ch):

> 'The principle is that encroachments by a tenant on land belonging to third parties will anomalously enure for the landlord's benefit provided that :
>
> (1) the land is "very close to the demised land and occupied by the tenant together with the demised land"; and
>
> (2) no different intention is shown by the conduct of the landlord or the tenant within the 12 years of adverse possession; the parties' acts subsequent to the expiry of the 12 year period are relevant

1 Land Registry, Practice Guide 4: Adverse Possession of Registered Land (January 2016) para 11.2.

2 Main Work at 13–03 ff. This is the approach suggested by the Law Commission, Law Com 227, at 17.86.

only in so far as they cast light on what the parties believed or intended at the end of that period.'

25–13A The Law Commission have helpfully set out the approach of the Land Registry in relation to encroachments by a tenant where the presumption has not been rebutted, as follows (paragraph 17.88):

> Land Registry's Practice Guide 4 provides that tenants who accept the presumption that the land is to be annexed to the lease can apply for first registration of leasehold title to the land. An application for registration is possible only where the tenant's lease has more than seven years to run, as leases for seven years or less are not registrable. Alternatively the tenant may apply for alteration of his or her existing title on the basis of the annexation of the land by encroachment.

25–14 There is conflicting authority as to whether the rebuttal must be manifested from the outset or whether it can be demonstrated at a later stage: *Doe D. Lewis v Rees* 6 Car & P 606; *Doe D. Lloyd v Jones* 15 M & W 579; *Andrews v Hailes* 2 El and Bl 347. It would appear that the intention has to be communicated to the landlord: *Doe D. Lloyd v Jones* 15 M & W 579; *Kingsmill v Millard* (1855) 19 JP 661.

25–26 A further illustration of the presumption being rebutted may be found in *Tickle v Admiral Taverns* REF/2012/0122.

25–40 Add to Fn 73: and also *Skipwith v Singh* REF/2009/850 at [12].

25–40A The authority of *Smirk* has however been doubted by both the minority and the majority in *Chau Ka Chik Tso*. For the minority Mr Justice Ribiero PJ stated as follows:

> '71. As indicated in Section A of this judgment, the original Government lease granting the relevant sections of the Lot to the respondents and their predecessors in title was for a term of 75 years from 1 July 1898 with a right of renewal for a further term of 24 years less the last three days. The 75 year portion of the term was therefore due to expire on 30 June 1973. This was the position affecting numerous leases since the Crown's practice, prior to 1959, had been to grant leases specifying an initial term of 75 years with the aforesaid right to renew.
>
> 72. On 9 May 1969, about four years before the initial term was due to expire, the Renewal Ordinance was passed.
>
> (a) Section 3 deals with the Ordinance's application:
>
> "This Ordinance applies to every Government lease existing immediately before the expiration of the 30th day of June 1973 under which land in the New Territories is demised for a term of seventy-five years from the 1st day of July 1898 and which contains a right of renewal for a further term of twenty-four years less three days, other than [certain immaterial exceptions]."
>
> (b) Section 4(2) deems the right to renew contained in the respondents' leases to have been duly exercised:

> "In the case of an existing Government lease of a lot which has been divided into sections before the 1st day of July 1973, the right of renewal contained in the lease shall be deemed to have been exercised by the persons entitled to that right and on that date there shall be deemed to be granted to such persons separate new Government leases of the land respectively held by them immediately before that date under the existing Government lease."

(c) Section 4(3) then sets out the terms of the renewed lease.

73. As Lord Nicholls of Birkenhead pointed out in *Chung Ping Kwan v Lam Island Development Co Ltd*, [55] one of the main purposes of the Renewal Ordinance was to avoid the administrative inconvenience of multiple renewal notices and multiple grants of new leases. Accordingly, as his Lordship there stated:

> "...the Ordinance should be approached on the footing that, save as otherwise provided, the Ordinance was intended to achieve the same result as would have occurred if a new lease had been granted pursuant to the right of renewal. The deemed new lease is to be regarded as having the like consequences in law as would have followed from an actual exercise of the renewal option and an actual grant of a new lease." [56]

74. That the deemed renewal under the Renewal Ordinance results in a new Government lease being granted was also recognized by Lord Hoffmann NPJ in *Chan Tin Shi v Li Tin Sung* [57]:

> "Section 4(1) of that Ordinance said that the options to renew in the existing leases should be deemed to have been exercised and that 'a new Government lease' should be deemed to have been granted. That undoubtedly created a new leasehold interest. Because the lease created by the option was a new estate, the Privy Council in *Chung Ping Kwan & Others v Lam Island Development Co Ltd* [1997] AC 38 had to consider whether adverse possession under the Limitation Ordinance barred not only the existing estate of the owner but also a new estate derived from a right which existed in the old lease."

75. It is this aspect of the Renewal Ordinance that Mr Edward Chan SC, appearing for the Government, emphasises. He relies on the passage in the judgment of Pennycuick VC in the *Smirk* decision discussed in Section B2.e above, for his contention that the break in the respondents' tenancies in 1973 prevented their acquisition of a leasehold interest in the encroachment area. I set out the passage again for convenience:

> "It seems to me, however, that the break in the tenancy necessarily negates [the claim that the tenant held the encroached upon land as an extension of the locus of his tenancy]. Whatever accrued or accruing right the plaintiff

may have had in 1968 to include the blue plot in his tenancy from British Railways, this right must have determined with his tenancy under British Railways, and obviously no new right can have accrued against the defendants during the short time in which they have been his landlords. There can be no ground for treating a period of two different tenancies as continuous for present purposes. Contrast the position where a possessory title is acquired by successive squatters, or against successive freeholders. The tenant, so long as the presumption applies, can do no more than acquire an addition to the subject matter of the tenancy and his interest in that additional subject matter must necessarily determine together with his interest in the original subject matter." [58]

76. This passage certainly suggests that Pennycuick VC thought that the tenant acquires no rights against his landlord where his holding is separable into two tenancies, with the initial tenancy being determined prior to expiry of the limitation period, followed by the grant of a fresh tenancy which has only run for a shorter time than the limitation period, even though the holding as tenant covers overall a continuous period exceeding the limitation period.

77. As previously indicated, I am unable to agree with that passage. It should be noted that, as Lawton LJ explained in the Court of Appeal, the possible relevance of a break in the tenancy was raised by Pennycuick VC only at the very end of the case, when counsel were making their final submissions. [59] No authority is cited for the proposition that such a break "necessarily negates" the claim to a leasehold interest pursuant to the encroachment doctrine. Nor is there any explanation as to why in principle a surrender and regrant of the tenancy, where occupation of the land encroached upon is seamless, should have such effect. The legal point was not explored in the Court of Appeal since their Lordships overturned Pennycuick VC's finding that there had been a break in the tenancy as a matter of fact.

78. Mr Chan SC relies on the passage as the basis for rejecting the respondents' claim to a leasehold interest over the encroached upon land. He submits that Pennycuick VC was right to recognize a "no adding up rule", that is, a rule whereby the Court refuses to add up the initial and renewed tenancy terms, treating them as continuous for the purposes of exceeding the limitation period in the context of the encroachment doctrine. Mr Chan submits that such a rule logically follows from what he calls "the coterminous rule", namely, the well established rule that any leasehold interest acquired under the doctrine by an encroaching tenant expires coterminously with his tenancy. Since, Mr Chan argues, a tenant whose occupation of an encroachment has matured into a leasehold interest must surrender up the land on expiry of his tenancy, a tenant whose tenancy has run for less than the limitation period ought

logically to be treated as having acquired nothing, and must set the clock ticking afresh under the subsequent tenancy. As Mr Chan puts it, the rights acquired by the encroaching tenant can only attach to a particular tenancy.

79. I cannot accept that argument. It appears to me to proceed on a mistaken view of the nature of the encroachment doctrine. Because of the presumption and the estoppel, the tenant is precluded from asserting that his occupation is by way of adverse possession and so prevents him from relying on the Limitation Ordinance against his landlord. In this way, the doctrine prevents the tenant from acquiring what might otherwise be the statutory rights flowing from adverse possession under the Ordinance. The leasehold interest acquired by the encroaching tenant is the result of applying the presumption and estoppel to both the tenant and the landlord under the doctrine. It does not depend on the tenant somehow "clocking up" time under an undivided tenancy as suggested by the "no adding up rule".

80. Even if, which I do not accept, acquisition of the leasehold interest depends upon the accrual of an uninterrupted period of time exceeding the limitation period, such accrual would have to relate to the period of occupation of the area of encroachment and not to the duration of the lease over the demised land. It would not depend or whether the tenancy of the adjacent demised land was granted under a single lease or under two back-to-back leases.

81. It therefore does not matter that the effect of the Renewal Ordinance was to determine the tenancy at the end of its original 75 year term and then immediately to deem a fresh tenancy granted for 24 years less the last three days. The respondents and their predecessors in title occupied the land encroached upon seamlessly for over 60 years. The doctrine therefore came into play, precluding any claim by the respondents based on adverse possession since they occupied the encroachment areas throughout as Government lessees and are presumed to have occupied those areas as an annex to their demised holdings, estopped from claiming otherwise.

82. The respondents are therefore entitled to a leasehold interest in the additional land. That interest is to be enjoyed until the end of their respective tenancies as Government lessees of the Lot. By operation of the New Territories Leases (Extension) Ordinance, [60] as explained in *Chan Tin Shi v Li Tin Sung*, [61] those tenancies terminate at the expiry of 30 June 2047.'

25–40B Lord Scott of Foscote NPJ for the majority's reasons were slightly different:

'The adding-up rule

124. Mr Chan submitted that the limitation period of 60 years that commenced in 1924 had been interrupted by the cesser on 30 June 1973 of the term of the original lease, that the period

had, perforce, to commence running afresh on 1 July 1973 when the further term of 24 years less 3 days commenced and that the period had not expired by December 2001 when the counterclaim for possession was served.

125. I am unable for a number of reasons to accept this submission. First, it seems to me unacceptably artificial to regard the Government as having acquired in 1924 a right of action to recover possession of the 6.67 acres that became spent on 30 June 1973 and as having acquired a fresh, identical right of action on 1 July 1973. The right of action acquired in 1924 was the same right of action, in respect of the same land, exercisable for the same reason, as the right of action exercisable on 1 July 1973. The notion that the deemed grant of the demised land made under s.4 of the 1969 New Territories (Renewable Government Leases) Ordinance had determined the original right of action and given rise to a new identical one seems to me misconceived. The trespass was the same wrongful act before and after 1 July 1973 and the potential right of action the Government had to remedy that wrongful act was the same right of action before and after that date.

126. Moreover, *Smirk v Lyndale Developments Ltd* [1975] Ch 317 is, in my opinion, the only authority of any weight that supports the notion that a period of adverse possession accrued under one lease cannot be added to a period of adverse possession accrued under its successor lease. This authority was naturally relied on by Mr Chan. It is, however, distinguishable. In *Smirk* there was no right of renewal included in the terms of the original tenancy. There was, therefore, at least an opportunity for the original lessor to determine the tenancy. In the present case, however, the original demise did contain a right of renewal and at no point of time did the lessor, the Government, have the ability to bring to an end the interest of any of the lessees in their respective sections. Even if the no adding-up rule for which *Smirk* stands as authority is good law, and I do not want to express an opinion on that, the rule seems to me inapplicable to a case where the original lease did confer a right of renewal and the right was duly exercised. In such a case the possession by a trespasser of encroached-upon land adjoining the land comprised in the original lease, who continues in that possession when the term granted by the original lease is renewed pursuant to a right of renewal contained in the original lease, does not, in my opinion, commence a new period of adverse possession when the new lease is granted. The reasons why not are explained by Lord Nicholls of Birkenhead in giving the judgment of the Privy Council in the *Chung Ping Kwan & Others v Lam Island Development Ltd* [1997] AC 38.'

25–42 The issue was further considered in *Hargreaves v Carus and Sons* [2015] UKFTT 0438 (PC).

Reform

25–49 Delete existing paragraph 25–49 and replace with:

The only proposals in Law Commission CP 227 were as follows: (at paragraph 17.86) that '*where a tenant is in adverse possession of land (other than land belonging to the landlord) and the presumption that the tenant is acting on behalf of his or her landlord is not rebutted, the landlord should be able to make an application under schedule 6 based on the tenant's adverse possession*'.

The contrary view is that the old law on encroachment should simply not be carried over into the Land Registration Act 2002 and the tenant should be entitled to claim in his own right. This is the view expressed by C Harpum in relation to these proposals.[1]

1 http://www.falcon-chambers.com/images/uploads/articles/Response_to_LC_CP_227_on_Land_Registration_%282%29.pdf

Chapter 29
Co-ownership

29–05 Add to Fn 6: *Lai Wai Kuen v Wong Shau Kwong* [2004] 4 HKC 528; *Tang Tak Sum v Tang Kai Fong* [2014] HKCA 584; *Chan Po King v Yau Wai Yin* [2015] HKCA 304.

29–09 Add to Fn 10: *King v Robertson* [2014] UKPC 34 (St Vincent) at [14] and [15].

Chapter 33

Boundaries

33–01 For boundary issues in general refer to Halsbury's Laws of England, Boundaries, Volume 4.

33–03 Add to Fn 1: since *Pennock*, the *Wibberly* case has been considered multiple times by the Court of Appeal: *Steward v Gallop* [2010] EWCA Civ 823; *Brown v Pretot* [2011] EWCA Civ 1421; *Dixon v Hodgson* [2011] EWCA Civ 1612; *Taylor v Lambert* [2012] EWCA Civ 3; *Hatton v Connew* [2013] EWCA Civ 1560; *Higson v Guenault* [2014] EWCA Civ 703; *Norman v Sparling* [2014] EWCA Civ 1152; a challenge to *Alan Wibberley* was rejected and the case approved in *Parmar & Others v Upton* [2015] EWCA Civ 795.

There may be further limits on the range of admissible evidence arising in relation to registered land, at least in relation to matters required to be put on the register: *Cherry Tree Investments Ltd v Landmain Ltd* [2012] EWCA Civ 736.

33–05 Add to Fn 5: and see the lively controversy in *Murdoch v Amesbury* [2016] UKUT 3 (TCC); *Bean v Katz* [2016] UKUT 168 (TCC) and *William Davis Ltd v Lowe* REF/2014/0573. See Chapter 21 of Law Commission CP 227 for the proposals to clarify the jurisdiction of the FTT.

33–06 Add to Fn 7: *Derbyshire County Council v Fallon* [2007] EWHC 1326 (Ch); *Drake v Fripp* [2011] EWCA Civ 1279.

33–09 Add to Fn 14: Since the last edition, the principal cases on *Ali* have been: *Kennerley v Beech* [2012] EWCA Civ 158; *Cameron v Boggiano* [2012] EWCA Civ 157; *Lanfearv Chandler* [2013] EWCA Civ 1497; *Norman v Sparling* [2014] EWCA Civ 1152; *Wood v Waddington* [2015] EWCA Civ 538; *Page v Convoy Investments Ltd* [2015] EWCA Civ 1061 (*obiter* statements about *Ali*), as well as some of those referred to in paragraph 33–03 above.

33–10 In a manner similar to the law relating to general boundaries, and the difference between so-called 'boundary' and 'title' cases, the law of boundary agreements has also evolved in a manner that distinguished between agreements that clarify the boundary on the one hand (and need not be in writing under s 2), and those which in truth amount to a disposal of land caught by s 2 and void if oral. The difference between the two categories of case is exceedingly difficult to draw save in the most obvious cases:

(1) In *Yeates v Line* [2012] EWHC 3085 (Ch), Mr Prosser QC (sitting as a Deputy High Court Judge) said:

'[29] *Joyce v Rigolli* is binding authority for the proposition that an oral demarcation agreement, that is an agreement to demarcate an unclear boundary described in title documents or delineated on a plan, is not void by virtue of section 2(1) of the 1989 Act even though the agreement has a disposing effect, because the words "a contract for..." in section 2(1) refer to an agreement which has a disposing purpose.

[35] Parliament has not impliedly enacted that a demarcation agreement need not comply with section 2(1): section 2(5) expressly excepts certain types of contract from the scope of the section, but demarcation agreements are not mentioned, and I do not think it is possible to imply a further exception. The reason why a demarcation agreement does not have to be in writing is simply because, as the Court of Appeal held in Joyce v Rigolli, the words "a contract for..." in section 2(1) refer to an agreement which has a disposing purpose, whereas a demarcation agreement does not have a disposing purpose. It may have a disposing effect, but this is "not the acid test", as Arden LJ put it. But if a disposing effect is not the acid test in relation to a boundary agreement, I do not see how it can be the acid test in relation to other agreements. After all, section 2(1) refers generally to "a contract" and "land", without distinguishing between boundary agreements and other agreements, or between a boundary and any other land, and I do not see how, even on a purposive interpretation, one can give the word "for" one meaning in relation to boundary agreements and a different meaning in relation to other agreements.

[36] It may be objected that this interpretation of section 2(1) conflicts with the aims of certainty, prevention of fraud, consumer protection, and so on, which are identified in the Law Commission Report, Formalities for Contracts for Sale Etc. of Land, and on which this legislation is based; and that in order to give effect to those aims I ought not to expand the categories of agreements which in fact dispose of land and which do not have to be in writing, beyond those contracts expressly mentioned in section 2(5) and demarcation agreements. But my task is to interpret section 2(1), and to do so in the light of the reasoning of the Court of Appeal in *Joyce v Rigolli*, and I consider that I am therefore required to decide that a demarcation agreement is no more than an example of an agreement which does not fall foul of section 2(1), because it does not have a disposing purpose even if it has a disposing effect. The compromise agreement in the present case is another example.'

(2) In *Nata Lee Ltd v Abid* [2014] EWCA Civ 1652, at [34], it was explained that 'where the purpose of an agreement was to delineate a boundary rather than to transfer land, it was to be presumed that any consequential transfer of land was trivial, unless the contrary

> was shown […] Again, the evidence and findings of the judge in the present case do not suggest that the purpose of the agreement was to define an uncertain boundary, but rather to transfer the disputed land.'

33–17A *Zarbv Parry* [2011] EWCA Civ 1306 is a further example of such a case.

33–29 Add to Fn 44: *Chow Tin Sang v Citihero Internation Limited* [2013] HKCA 301.

Chapter 35

Licences and tenancies at will

35–10 Unfortunately none of the criticism of BP were considered by the Privy Council in *Smith v Molyneaux (British Virgin Islands)* [2016] UKPC 35.

35–47A The *Alston* approach was endorsed by the Court of Appeal in *Zarb v Parry* [2011] EWCA Civ 1306, Arden LJ explaining that there had to be unequivocal evidence of consent. Here, there were general statements by the paper title owner and the erection of a fence by which the paper title owner excluded himself from part of his own land. Arden LJ stated as follows:

> '[27] The crucial question is whether the acts and words of Mr Little were "probative of and not merely consistent with the giving of permission". The judge made no finding about the evidence of Mrs Zarb regarding the alleged statement by Mrs Ceen and, in any event, permission to play on the Strip is hardly probative of an intention to give the right to possession of it.
>
> [28] The erection of that fence is wholly equivocal: it did not mean that Mr Little consented to the Parrys having possession of the Strip. Mr Little might well just have erected that fence for some other purpose, for example to stop his stock from damaging the hedge or going through it and thence into (any part of) the garden of the Ceens. As HHJ Marshall QC made clear in *J Alston & Sons Ltd v BOCM* [2009] 1 EGLR 93, mere acquiescence in another's use of one's land is not the same as the grant of permission for that user for the purposes of the stopping time running in favour of an adverse possessor.'

35–47B In *Smart v Lambeth LBC* [2013] EWCA Civ 1375, the squatter, S, was occupying a house. The house belonged to the local authority, Lambeth. Lambeth had implemented a policy whereby squatters should form housing co-operatives. A scheme was then devised whereby Lambeth would grant a licence to a housing association, which would in turn licence the housing co-operative, which would in turn allow squatters to reside in the houses in question. The co-operative was obliged to grant licences in a particular form. Although prior occupiers had entered into such licences, S never did and claimed that therefore, he was a squatter entitled to possession. The Court of Appeal did not refer to the *Alston* decision or to the difficulties with the *Rumbelow* test, though did consider the authorities set out in paragraph 35–46 of the Main Work. The Court of Appeal decided that, when S took possession, there were sufficient circumstances from which it could be concluded that possession was under the terms of the scheme which had been implemented and that he must therefore have known that he was there with permission. Further, Lambeth had given a global licence to occupy, so that, vis-a-vis Lambeth, it did not matter that the precise procedure in the licence with the housing co-operative had not been complied with.[1]

35–47C Although *Smart* is consistent also with what is respectfully suggested to be the proper test in *Beresford* (paragraph 35–32 of the Main Work), particularly by reason of S's participation in the workings of the housing co-operative, the reasoning in *Smart* appears unsound in light of the failure to consider *Beresford* and *Alston*. Further, it is not clear that Lambeth were in fact licensing the individual squatters – rather, it would appear that the licence was only granted to the housing association and onward to the housing co-operative. It is not clear, therefore, how S (or any other eventual occupier) became privy to the benefit of the underlying Lambeth licence. It is considered that the *Smart* case could have been decided on the alternative basis that, whilst the licence between Lambeth and the housing association, and the subordinate licence between the housing association and the co-operative, remained in force, time could not in fact run against Lambeth, as it had no presently vested claim for possession against S. This would have produced the same result.[2]

35–47D Unfortunately, the relevant test was not considered by the Privy Council in *Smith v Molyneaux* [2016] UKPC 35. Although it would not have made a difference to the outcome, the failure to consider the development of the test through the cases cited above resulted in the Privy Council citing *BP Properties Ltd v Buckler* (1988) 55 P & CR 337 with uncritical approval.

35–49 Contrast however *Mitchell v Watkinson* [2014] EWCA Civ 1472, at [75]–[82], where three trustees of a cricket club held an oral periodic tenancy of fields used by the club. They stopped paying rent, meaning that time ran against the freeholder. Before the expiry of the limitation period, the last of the trustees died intestate, and his estate vested in the Probate Judge. The Court of Appeal held that the Probate Judge succeeded to the tenancy and was in possession of the disputed land through the members of the club, who both before and after the death of the last of the trustees to die, occupied the land pursuant to a contractual licence. There is, accordingly, a distinction to be drawn between a revocable bare licence and a contractual licence, the latter taking effect as a true contract and continuing to bind the deceased's estate. As to the effect of death, see further *To Wai Sing v To Hung Tai* [2014] HKCA 381; and *Smith v Molyneaux* [2016] UKPC 35 where it was seemingly assumed that the death of the *licensee* would have terminated the licence, though that aspect of the decision may have turned on the facts.

---

1 And the Court of Appeal decided correctly that the fact that the licence was not in accordance with a contract did not render it void: see at [34].

2 And see *Mann, R (on the application of) v Somerset County Council* [2012] EWHC B14 (Admin), in which the Divisional Court expressed the view that there was no material difference between *Beresford* on the one hand, and *Zarb v Parry* [2011] EWCA Civ 1306 at [64]–[66].

Index